The Adobe Story is an outgrowth of a senior education and service experience called the New Mexico Adobe Mission Project. It was developed as an experimental model for providing development education by Helen Kerschner, Ph.D., President of the American Association for International Aging (AAIA), and Executive Director of the University of New Mexico Center on Aging. One of the primary goals of the project was to experiment with an innovative method for incorporating international issues into a seemingly domestic education and service program. Two project objectives were: (1) to educate Americans and share the information and experience common to other peoples of the world, in order to honor and rescue an almost lost art; and (2) to develop a bridge of mutual interests with our international neighbors through education and involvement, in a shared experience that all can understand and appreciate.

The first Adobe Mission Project took place in the summer of 1993. The AAIA, in cooperation with the University of New Mexico Center on Aging provided transportation, camping equipment, and food for the participants. Buzz McHenry prepared an educational curriculum, and a work program for the Center on Aging at the University of New Mexico. The Center recruited participants and organized the project. Fifteen older adults and teenage students participated in a restoration project at a mission in *Ojo Caliente* (literally translated hot eye, but meaning a hot spring). It involved two days of education about the implications of adobe around the world, four days of restoration work on an old adobe mission (while camping out in a local spa), and one day of touring historic adobe structures in northern New Mexico.

A second effort was organized in 1994. It included twenty older adults and high school students in a similar education and service program that lasted four days. The addition to this project was fireside chats with Buzz in the evenings.

A new on-going Adobe Mission Project is now being undertaken. It includes both retirees and students from the University of New Mexico, and will provide both education and community service opportunities. It is being undertaken in conjunction with on-going restoration activities at *Rancho de Las Golandrinas* (ranch of the swallows), a living history site that was a stopping place on *El Camino Real* (the royal road) from Mexico City to Santa Fe.

Those who cannot participate in a New Mexico Adobe Mission Project will enjoy a fascinating experience in reading:

THE ADOBE STORY: A Global Treasure

THE ADOBE STORY: A Global Treasure

by Paul G. McHenry, Jr.

with a foreword by
Helen K. Kerschner, Ph.D.
President of the American Association for International Aging
Director, Center for Aging, University of New Mexico

This book is published by
The American Association for International Aging
Washington, DC
and
Center for Aging, University of New Mexico
Albuquerque, NM

ACKNOWLEDGMENTS

This book would not have been possible without the help of the hundreds of people that I have worked with over the past fifty years. They have been willing to give their time and share their skills and philosophy with me. It would be impossible to name them all, but I want to include my father, Bud Litchke, Jim Davies, and Lloyd Gambling. Also, I would be remiss to omit my friends at Acoma, Taos, Santa Ana, and the other Pueblos.

Helen Kerschner, Director of the UNM Center for Aging, planted the idea for this and then helped it grow. Her thoughtful input gave direction to the subject. Gregory Lay and my son James, my editors, asked questions about paragraphs that I thought were perfectly clear but were not. They also corrected my grammar and punctuation. My wife Carol, whose support was vital, was understanding and patient with me. Our son James, with his photography and computer skills, not only dealt with the technical challenges, but displayed his artistic talents in the design of the book. Last but not least, I'd like to thank the AAIA and USAID for their generous financial contributions. Thank you all for your help.

Paul McHenry

3 1472 70072 0836

THE ADOBE STORY
by Paul G. McHenry
Text Copyright © American Association for International Aging 1996
Photos Copyright © Paul G. McHenry 1996
Albuquerque, New Mexico, USA

First Edition 1996

Published by the American Association for International Aging, 1900 L St. NW, #510, Washington, DC 20036
Book design, electronic layout, and Kodak PhotoCD™ image manipulation by James McHenry Intermedia
http://www.nmia.com/~jgm

Library of Congress Cataloging-in-Publication Data
McHenry, Paul G. 1924-
THE ADOBE STORY: A Global Treasure
1. Adobe Buildings, 2. Earth Buildings, 3. Earth Architecture

foreword

Before I moved to New Mexico, I had heard of a wonderful architect who was often referred to as "Mr. Adobe." Not long after I arrived, I managed to catch up with Paul (Buzz) McHenry on the campus of the University of New Mexico and we began what turned out to be a wonderful collaboration in education and action.

I was intrigued with Buzz' energy and experience in adobe architecture and his global view of adobe. He was intrigued with my interest in organizing education programs for older adults and encouraging their involvement in service. Together, we built on a theme of "acting locally...thinking globally" by developing a domestic education/service program with international implications. The purpose was to praise the esoteric art, yet pass on the useful traditions...to describe the practical methods, yet document the technological changes...to appreciate the domestic contradictions, yet address the global consistencies.

My experience working with Buzz has resulted in an enormous appreciation of adobe. Our visits to the Governor's Palace in Santa Fe, to the Sun Dwellings of Ghost Ranch, to the Mosque in Abiquiu, and to the remote monastery on the Chama River have provided an understanding of the beauty of simplicity...a simplicity without the encumbrance of time or place. His collection of thousands of slides of adobes from countries around the world have helped me understand why Buzz calls adobe "the common bond of our global community."

His lectures have helped me understand that while, historically, the United States has been a follower, it now must assume leadership in the preservation of both the art and the architecture.

As you read <u>THE ADOBE STORY: A Global Treasure</u>, you will see why students and faculty at the University and adobe builders in the U.S. and all around the world are intrigued with Buzz and his love of adobe. When he talks about using adobe because it can be economical as well as energy and environmentally efficient, you will see the implications for our own diminishing resources as well as those of other countries. You will also see why his lectures to and consultations with the global community call for recommitting ourselves to sustainable development by "building with the dirt under our feet."

So I invite you to enjoy Buzz' tour of the adobe experience...the past and the present...the standard and the upscale...the domestic and the global. I can assure you that your experience will be entertaining and educational. I have no doubt that you will come away with a new appreciation that comes from visiting with an expert...and Buzz is the expert...both in working with adobe and living in it.

Helen K. Kerschner

Dr. Kerschner is Director of the University of New Mexico Center on Aging and Executive Director of the American Association for International Aging (AAIA). This Second Edition of <u>The Adobe Story, A Global Treasure</u> was printed courtesy of AAIA. The First Edition, which was prepared and printed in 1966, was funded through AAIA's Development Education for Retired Americans Project, a project made possible by the generous support of the United States Agency for International Development.

preface

I had been lecturing on adobe architecture to a wide variety of groups at UNM for several years, including several programs of the UNM Center For Aging. Helen Kerschner, Director of the center proposed the idea of a group actually doing some hands-on field work on a real building. Of all the groups, I enjoy the seniors most. They are, almost without exception, the brightest, most enthusiastic people I know. They are tireless.

Northern New Mexico has an almost endless supply of old adobe buildings needing repair, so there were many buildings from which to choose. We selected an old Church at Ojo Caliente that had been de-consecrated by the Archdiocese several years earlier, but was revered by the community, who wanted it repaired.

One of my first concerns was the hard physical part of working with adobe. This problem was solved by the addition of some teen-agers, who added a much larger dimension to the whole experience than we expected. They actually talked to the seniors. Both parts of the group benefited greatly from the dialog and experience of working together.

My background in adobe and other forms of earthen building covers more than 35 years and almost all parts of the globe. A common denominator found worldwide was adobe. This is a forsaken material in much of the modern world, but we are returning to it because the developing nations have no other choice. If we look back at the past 75 years of our history, we see countless examples of adobe coming to the rescue when small towns needed churches and schools and did not have the financial resources to pay for them. The dirt is free, and it is labor intensive so it provides work.

Hopefully this book will expand the understanding of how earth has been and can be used in times of economic hardship. If this provides a common bond between nations on a very basic level, I will feel this book has been a success.

Paul G. McHenry

Contents

ADOBE: A DEFINITION

The word adobe is in wide use in the United States of America and Spanish speaking countries. It can mean adobe bricks, the soil that used to make them, the mud plaster, the building that is built of adobe bricks, and the architectural style, which has several sub-divisions.

The word itself is believed to come from the Arabic *at-tubah*, which means "the brick." The "adobe" style of architecture migrated from North Africa to Spain, so the name adobe must have come with it. In many other countries, the word adobe is meaningless, and it is more accurate to say "earthen brick." Other forms of the same material with different names, such as rammed earth, *Pise, Jacal, Barjareque*, or puddled mud are sometimes referred to as adobe.

chapter one
Adobe is a Magic Material

Most people in the United States associate adobe with grand haciendas in the sun drenched deserts of New Mexico and Arizona, creating a romantic image of a magic place with cowboys, Indians, and long vistas of desert with distant mountains. Much of this image was generated by the advertising campaigns of the Santa Fe Railroad and the Fred Harvey Houses, with their posters showing natives with big hats, wrapped in blankets, sleeping against the sunny side of a building.

Unfortunately some people tend to relate the word adobe to shabby, country dwellings and poverty. The name Santa Fe brings up an image of narrow crooked streets, quaint shops and restaurants, and a community dedicated to art and artists. The city of Santa Fe represents the adobe image for the world and wealthy immigrants from other parts of the United States who come there have turned this simple material into one representing luxury and high cost.

WORLDWIDE USE

Although most people think of mud buildings only in a desert setting, the earthen material used for buildings, called adobe, are found the world over, in many unlikely places. Early shelter consisted of caves and sun drenched cliffs that were protected from the wind. People later began creating shelter from simple materials at hand. Similar techniques for building shelter were developed independently in many parts of the world. Dates when this work was taking place may differ by centuries, with buildings representing the cultural level at that place, at that time. One of the first simple dwelling forms to use adobe mud was the "pit house." It was partially below ground, used a wood framework for walls and roof, and was then plastered with mud to seal out the weather. Remains of these can be found in New Mexico, Arizona, and portions of Northern Mexico. This form was so satisfactory that there was virtually no change in the basic pattern for more than 600 years.

Adobe is an incredibly versatile material! It can be used to make bricks and plaster, piled it up in the form of a wall, or to fill the spaces between logs and brush. It is also waterproof to some degree, and can be used for roofing.

What first captures the imagination is the possibility that an elegant home can be built with the materials under your feet. Psychologists speak of a "nesting" instinct that is in everyone to create a shelter. It starts in childhood with cardboard boxes in the backyard and is found in all ages. Adobe offers the opportunity to indulge this to the utmost degree and by doing it ourselves, we can create a home that we could not otherwise afford.

The sensation of living in an adobe home is solid, quiet, secure, and peaceful. It is difficult to explain, and it must be experienced to be truly understood. The quiet can be disturbing to some. In most conventional homes, we are marginally aware of what is going on outside, like shouting, music, or car sounds.

The skills to build with adobe are simple. Mix soil with water, mold it into bricks, and let them dry in the sun. Mix more soil and water for mortar to glue the bricks and stack them up. It is really that simple. Adobe is a strong material, except for its vulnerability to water, which really is of relatively minimum concern. The clay provides resistance to rainfall and the walls can last for centuries. It is a forgiving material, and it is difficult to build so badly that it won't be successful. If the wall falls over, simply pick up the bricks and use them again. If the brick pieces get too small to use, throw them in the mud pit and make new bricks from them. Adobe is a material that recycles itself!

The simplicity of the technology is difficult for people who are used to more complex systems where specialists are needed for the simplest tasks.

The principles of shelter were developed from the lessons learned using caves and cliff shelters. The typical shelter had to have protection from the weather and some degree of comfort, the same elements we look for today. The conception and discovery of more sophisticated forms and materials led to more complex forms such as arches and vaults. In some areas, most notably in the Middle East, earth building techniques were used to achieve magnificent monuments and raised simple adobe masonry to a complex art form.

The technology is so similar the world over, that it can be difficult to identify the geographic location of a particular photo. The following photos illustrate and compare the shared resource of adobe in several parts of the world.

GUESS WHERE THE FOLLOWING PICTURES WERE TAKEN:

A rural home in western China. The triangle brick pattern on the wall is universal. This pattern increases the height of the wall and adds a decorative element. The hay on the roof serves as insulation in the winter, and prevents the livestock from eating more than the allotted share.

An unoccupied home in Hillsboro, New Mexico, USA. It appears that it was never plastered on the exterior, but still provided snug shelter. The doors and windows are intact, indicating a continuing interest by the owner. If a building is truly abandoned, the first elements to be salvaged are the doors and windows.

A typical home in Cyprus. This scene could have been taken almost anywhere in New Mexico or Latin America. The *"horno"* oven and protruding roof beams are common the world over.

A country home in Bolivia. The *horno* oven not only bakes bread, but keeps the chickens warm. Straw, a traditional ingredient for adobe, can be seen in the mud plaster covering the oven.

ADOBE HAS BEEN FORSAKEN

Adobe seems to be a forsaken material in the eyes of the world. After millenniums of dependable use in almost every climate and condition Mother Nature can throw at mankind, we have turned our back on adobe. Can we be so foolish as to let our devotion to modern materials deprive us of what we need? Surely not!

Most of today's professionals - architects, engineers, government officials, and contractors have been educated by western standards or in western institutions and have lost touch with the material of the common people. People have a love affair with modern materials, and often equate "old" with "shabby," unless it has some historical importance. Many old buildings have been saved only by this "historical importance," while others with equally strong walls have been demolished to make room for new styles and materials. If we look at the early basic housing technology as a logical use of readily available resources, our own housing shortages could be diminished. The old skills, barely alive, are in danger of being lost if we don't make an active effort to preserve and encourage them.

Many years ago, at an international housing conference in Brussels, Belgium, the best known advocate of earthen housing, Egyptian architect Hassan Fathy, suggested adobe as a partial solution for the international housing problem. He was not only scorned, but vilified and threatened by short sighted foes who ignored the energy, ecology, and logical considerations. They typified his work as a "return to the Middle Ages."

Iran palace tower. This elegant palace is an example of the luxurious end of the adobe spectrum. After the masonry has been repaired, the mud plaster will be replaced. The height of the wind tower (built with adobe) would be prohibited in the United States by buildings codes. Yazd, Iran

Unbelievably, this type of attitude is all too common with professionals unfamiliar with earth buildings. The communication systems of today often make the American standard of living the goal for every remote corner of the globe. Because of this, the people who are most in need of housing often view earth buildings with disdain as well.

The "poverty image" unfortunately is firmly fixed in the minds of many people in the world, and they are amazed at the beautiful things being done with adobe in New Mexico. I gave a slide show of some of New Mexico's adobe homes, for the Architecture School students in Lima, Peru. They were amazed at the quality and beauty of the homes, and even more amazed at the idea that adobe was a luxury material that only the wealthy could afford.

Elegant Santa Fe house. The quiet dignity of this home overlooking the Rio Grande Valley needs no further explanation of its quality. Santa Fe, New Mexico, USA

A number of years ago, the City of Tucson razed a large portion of their "old town" Victorian houses that were in the way of new city downtown development, and discovered to their surprise that they were made of adobe bricks. This use of adobe bricks was widespread and not limited to Tucson. Since the word adobe evokes Pueblo Style in the minds of most people, its use as a "regular" brick for other styles comes as a surprise.

chapter two
Shelter Around the World

Food and shelter are the two basic human needs. They have common denominators in all parts of the world. Specific conditions, attitudes, and reactions about building materials vary with country, culture, and age. Attitudes perhaps play a more significant role than we realize. The expression "a proper house" used in describing the features necessary for a house will vary from country to country and culture to culture. What is "proper" to one group may mean nothing to another. It is also subject to generational influences. Some features like fine furnishings that one generation considered desirable may have less appeal to their children. Architectural perceptions, like beauty, lie in the eye of the beholder. In most of Europe, housing was built to last "forever," and many habitations are centuries old. Certain patterns have developed, for example, where leaseholds are a way of life. The thought of buying and owning a particular dwelling may be foreign to many Europeans, and sometimes a leasehold will be occupied by the same family for centuries. In turn, the owner expects the property to be a permanent responsibility and source of income.

The attitude of the average North American places great expectations on buying and owning a dwelling for at least their own lifetime, but not necessarily that of their children. Coupled with the mobility of today's work force, this creates quite a different attitude. An examination and understanding of these attitudes offers a bridge on which to exchange and explore new ideas. The comparison and discovery of universal ideals could lead to an exchange of ideas that would promote better understanding and good will between the peoples of the world.

Today, it has been said, more than half of the world's population live in shelters made of earth. It has always been that way. Most early efforts to provide shelter, millenniums ago, took into account the elements of the climate, protected the shelter from the wind, and warmed it from the sun.

Caves have been carved from the soft tufa (solidified volcanic ash) cliffs, and further extended by the use of shaped tufa blocks or adobe bricks. Puyé Cliffs, New Mexico, USA

The forms were simple representations of the builder's experience of what was most comfortable, and the use of materials that were readily at hand. Other factors influencing shelter location were proximity of food and water. When the number of people exceeded the food supply or climatic changes decreased the water supply, inhabitants abandoned their dwellings and moved to a location where these were adequate.

Anthropology traces man's origin and development by identifying unique skills or features that have been transferred from one area of the world to another. Earthen buildings seem to have developed independently in most parts of the world and the embodied principles are repeated. The forms and techniques are basically the same. After a time, as we will see in photos, many features and styles are almost identical, even though separated by vast oceans. A typical element is the functional and effective "claustra," where adobe bricks are laid at an angle in the wall to form a series of open triangles. This provides a screen for privacy, but at the same time, allows light and ventilation. An example can be seen in the photo on page 3.

The pace of these developments was not the same for all parts of the world, but all were developed along the same principles in response to available resources and climate. There are countless surviving examples to be found everywhere.

Adobe is the most common building material in rural areas. The techniques of adobe construction are well known to most of the country farmers. Tarija, Bolivia

BUILDING WITH EARTH

Shelter can be built with nothing more than soil, water, and our hands. The guiding principle for adobe builders is to use what is at hand, keep it simple, and do it yourself. The soil under our feet provides the basic material. Trees obtained from the closest source serve as roof beams. Stone helps reinforce foundations, corners, and places where the adobe might be subject to damage.

In the past century, in the western United States at least, nearly everybody had the basic skills and resourcefulness to build what was needed, whether it was a barn, house, school, or church. The sophisticated and specialized resources of today were nonexistent then, and people had to make do with what they had around them, or do without. Many rural people today still have this skill and resourcefulness.

This small, rural community needed a larger elementary school in 1941 and had few financial resources. Adobe provided the answer: economical local material and local labor who needed employment. Anthony, New Mexico, USA

When a church was needed in this remote mountain mining community, adobe was the answer. Pinos Altos, New Mexico, USA

Current builders in the industrial world who recognize the advantages of earthen buildings and would like to acquire the skills must learn the lessons that developed the technology as our ancestors did. Much of it is by trial and error. Separating myth from reality is the first task in understanding this material. The use of earth for building has been a native craft for so many years that many myths and traditions have been established. Special soils from particular places are sometimes believed to be necessary. Certain additives are credited with being necessary or giving the bricks special qualities.

My own experience is a case in point. In the early 1960s, after ten years in the practice of conventional construction, I became intrigued with the idea of building with adobe. I bought a piece of property and looked in the library for written material to tell me how to build with adobe. The only reference readily available was one book by a couple in California that designed and built their own home of adobe. As adobe construction was going on currently in New Mexico, and with few library resources available, the logical source for information would be the adobe brick makers. The first one told me that he had the only good soil for adobes (which happened to be on his grandfather's property). This didn't make sense, so I checked with another brick-maker in another community who said his was the only good soil. He also had a special ingredient that made it strong... The manure from his black horse in the corral!

Unfortunately, these myths are rampant in the adobe business, so one has to look at all of these statements with care, using logic and good sense. In all fairness, there is sometimes a certain scientific validity to many of these self serving myths. Throughout the world, straw is added to the soil if the clay content is too high, so the bricks will not develop shrinkage cracks when drying. Most naturally occurring soils have too much clay, hence the straw myth. The manure may add a chemical or physical element that makes that particular soil work.

The use of earth and water was the earliest form of "built" housing and it was developed simultaneously in many parts of the world. If the basics of dwellings are understood, common elements can be identified with the rest of the world, providing a common bond that can foster international understanding.

There are three basic types of earthen construction:

ADOBE, RAMMED EARTH, AND JACAL

ADOBE   Adobe is made from dirt and water, molded into bricks, and dried by the sun. This is mostly used in arid lands or in areas where there is a dry period of several weeks without rain, to allow the bricks to cure. This doesn't mean desert necessarily, but there must be one or more relatively rain free periods during the year. Adobe brick buildings are found in all climates. Examples from around the world show similarities and the diversity of form.

An *adobero* makes three bricks at a time, mining the soil from a local river bed. After drying, these will be fired like pottery in a simple wood fired kiln. These bricks then become "burned adobes", that are erosion resistant. A current problem for this brick factory is that all of the locally available firewood for a distance of 25 kilometers has been consumed. Production can be 300 bricks per day. Sasabe, Mexico

Brick-making in an adobe production yard using material handling equipment and "ladder" forms for mass production. Special equipment includes a "pug" mill and large front bucket loaders. Production can reach 7,000 per day. Albuquerque, New Mexico, USA

An adobe home under construction. Concrete foundations rise above the ground level to prevent moisture from rising into the adobe walls. The corners are built first, plumb and square, to provide a reference point for the walls in between. Corrales, New Mexico, USA

Where wood is in short supply, or virtually nonexistent, arches and barrel vaults of adobe are used for the floor or roof of the house above. Mud plaster covers the bricks. Faruj, Iran

Intricate patterns of intersecting domes and vaults of adobe brick are sometimes sheathed with fired brick or ceramic tile to protect them from the weather. Dervish Mosque, Mahan, Iran

One of the most surprising examples of adobe brick buildings in unlikely places was from Rochester, New York (ca. 1850). At an international conference in Las Cruces, New Mexico in 1990, a group of architects from New York showed photos of more than 25 adobe houses. All appear to be surviving well today in the state of New York.

Adobe brick building in Geneva, New York USA. Photo courtesy R. Pieper, Architect, New York, USA

RAMMED EARTH

Rammed earth, *pise* or *tapial* as it is also called, is a wall shaped of damp earth, compacted, and allowed to dry. Most often, wooden forms are used to contain the soil while it is compacted. It is used in climatic areas where there is not enough continuous sunshine to dry adobe bricks. It is not uncommon to find rammed earth wall construction in the same vicinity or even the same building as adobe bricks. This is probably a cultural matter, where the preferences are a matter of experience and tradition of a particular individual.

An earth building of several stories has been in use for many years in the South of France. (Building codes in the United States limit the height of adobe buildings to two stories or less.) North of Annecy, France

The Church of the Holy Cross, ca. 1850, was built of rammed earth, and has survived earthquakes and hurricanes for more than a century. Stateburg, South Carolina, USA. Photo courtesy The Church of the Holy Cross

Even simpler methods are used in the Middle East, making earth walls by shaping damp earth by hand, and pressing it into a wall shape without the need for forms.

A wall of packed earth serves for garden walls in Iran. No forms are used, but mud is mixed at the base of the wall, placed and shaped by hand, layer on layer, like coil pottery. Faruj, Iran

Casas Grandes, a ruin of a prehistoric city in the state of Chihuahua, Mexico, was built of "puddled" earth in the 11th century AD. Puddled construction uses a wetter mixture than is used in rammed earth. The mixture must be stiff enough to hold its shape without slumping. Note the similarities to the previous photo. Casas Grandes, Chihuahua, Mexico

A multi-storied rammed earth apartment house. Weilberg, Germany. Photo courtesy Lydia Miller, the Rammed Earth Institute, Greely, Colorado, USA

In China, logs are used for forms, contained by temporary posts. When the logs are removed, the wall has a corrugated appearance. This type of wall construction is common throughout China.

Rammed Earth wall formed with logs. Near Xi'an, China

JACAL Jacal, also called wattle and daub or *bajareque*, is mud placed over a wood and brush framework. Vertical posts are placed in the ground, horizontal branches and brush are fastened to or woven on the posts, and the whole framework covered with mud to keep out the rain and wind. The earliest forms of these were called "pit houses," and were partially sunken in the ground. This was a favored house form of the Hohokam Indians of northern Mexico and the southwestern United States. The below ground feature utilized the natural warmth of the earth (±55 degrees f.), and the clay in the mud provided waterproofing for the walls and roof. By placing the excavated soil directly on the wall, it was very labor effective in moving the soils a minimum distance. This form of shelter is found worldwide.

Another form of underground house is also found in limited areas. The underground house is actually excavated from a very solid compact soil formation that is strong enough to resist collapse. It might be likened to carving a cave out of an adobe brick hundreds of feet thick. This is found in central China and North Africa.

Museum model of a Hohokam "pit house," a type that is common in much of the world. Casa Grande National Monument, Casa Grande, Arizona, USA

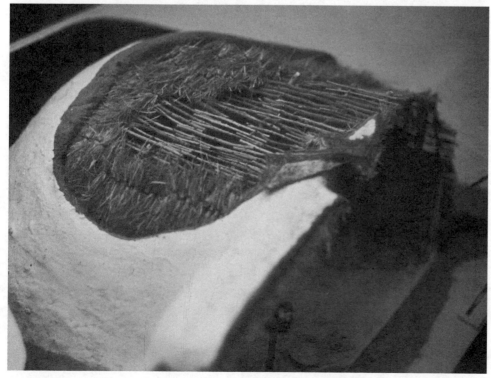

Museum model showing roof details. Casa Grande National Monument, Casa Grande, Arizona, USA

Many rural buildings were built using this palisade type construction. Sharpened poles are inserted in a "V" groove beam at the top. This supports the roof structure and the wall is covered with mud plaster. Frequently, this type building is mistaken for an adobe building. Chama River farm building, near Abiquiu, New Mexico, USA

The case for using earth for building may be summed up as follows:

❖ All you have to do is look for the nearest, simple material.
❖ Most of the remaining skilled earth builders may not be very articulate. Many are simple people who have little formal education but are skilled builders with earth. We can learn many practical lessons from them.
❖ Many professionals of today tend to ignore these hard won skills.
❖ As a result, earth building has been in decline for a number of decades. Building with adobe is a dying art, a trend that must be reversed if we are to meet the world's housing needs. We can learn by examining the past to see how things were done in simpler times.

chapter three
Living in Art

Adobe is a warm and sensuous material that can be a sculptural art form. It can also lend itself to conventional building patterns when used as a common masonry material. Its abstract shapes are limited only by the imagination of the builder. In the more artistic forms, it can be a sensory experience of total immersion in a piece of sculpture. Each space is unique, and turning each corner brings a new experience and sometimes a delightful surprise.

The forms can vary from the conventional style rectangular buildings, to intricate geometric patterns, and into the realm of abstract shapes that are pleasing to the eye. Islamic tradition frowns on the depiction of human or animal figures. This led to a concentration on geometric design and calligraphy. The structural elements of many Islamic architecture examples include the artistic design elements as well.

FROM THE TRADITIONAL TO THE ABSTRACT

A favorite feature of adobe homes, new or old, is the inclusion of architectural antiques. The stair railing shown here was hand crafted many years ago in another country, salvaged and relocated to provide an unusual feature in the restoration and reconstruction of this fine home. Santa Fe, New Mexico, USA

A two story apartment house of adobe in a modified Greek Revival style, ca. 1915, was razed to make room for a new housing project. Albuquerque, New Mexico, USA

City apartment and store buildings of adobe. The traditional pattern of shops at street level with living quarters above still prevails in many parts of the world. Note the graceful arches over the windows and simple geometric design integrated in the masonry. Tehran, Iran, 1972

Sculptured adobe fireplace in a modern home. The curved forms of the firebox opening are repeated in the fireplace face, and in the integrated banco for seating. P.G. McHenry, Architect. Albuquerque, New Mexico, USA

The building form presented here reflects two influences. One is the low, informal main building massed in the Pueblo style, and then a church bell tower spire whose irregular form is in harmony with the main building. Native American Church, Albuquerque, New Mexico, USA

In the more traditional, or "expected" form of the Pueblo style, traditional examples illustrate the sculptural qualities. In most architecture, form follows function, limited to the sizes and shapes of the material. Adobe lets the builder create the form in a shape that is pleasing to him. The "art" and beauty of adobe architecture lies in the spontaneity felt by the builder. The design and form feels right, and is not the product of a rule or formula.

The traditional Pueblo Style is typified in Taos Pueblo. The building masses are clustered for defense, and have terraces which serve as outdoor living spaces and defensive platforms. In this style the *vigas* (roof beams) frequently protrude from the wall, possibly indicating a reluctance to cut off a structural member whose length might be used in another location. Taos Pueblo, New Mexico, USA, 1946

chapter four
Earthwalls for All Climates

Man has always managed to find ways to use earth for building shelter in all parts of the globe, with variations to suit each particular climate. The ingenuity of man meets the challenges posed by the local environment.

Masonry skills that were developed in the arid lands of the Middle East are truly mind boggling. In a climate where there is virtually nothing but sand, soil, intermittent streams, and only periodic rainfall, man's ingenuity was pushed to the limit.

The original notion that enabled man to build roofs over large buildings using small pieces of mud masonry as structural members is almost beyond belief. These examples attest to the ability of the human race to adapt to almost any environment.

ADAPTATIONS

DESERT REGIONS

Village view from minaret. The entire village is built of mud brick, using arches, domes, and vaults for roofing. The large building in the background is a former fort that has been in continuous use since 400 BC. Faruj, Iran

The weight of this person standing on a 10 inch thick barrel vault of adobe brick shows it's surprising strength. Faruj, Iran

This palace and wind tower are being restored. The *bad gir* (wind catcher) scoops will send air to the basement to be cooled by the lower temperatures of the earth, and will circulate upwards through vents in the floors. The heated exhaust air is drawn out on the downwind side of the wind catcher. Palace near Yazd, Iran

In damp, rainy climates it may not be possible to make adobe bricks, because of the lack of dry periods long enough to cure the bricks. In this event, rammed earth can be used.

HUMID CLIMATES

Rammed earth farmhouse. As the weakest part of an earth wall is at the corners, angled cement reinforcements are placed there to reinforce that part of the wall. The surface is not plastered, but protected by the roof overhang. Near Lyon, France

A multi-storied rammed earth warehouse. Villifontaine, France

Rammed earth is favored by some cultures, even when the climate is suitable for adobe bricks, and the two forms are often found side by side with no conflict.

An outstanding example of adobe brick construction in a damp, humid, earthquake prone area is the Carmel High School, built of asphalt stabilized adobes in 1938. Current building codes in California are very restrictive in allowing the use of adobe for building. In spite of the discouraging policy against the use of adobe, many old adobe buildings still exist in California that have survived centuries of weather and earthquakes. Unfortunately, a lack of understanding of this time tested material seems prevalent worldwide.

This photo of Carmel High School taken in 1995, more than 50 years after its construction, shows that adobe is not a fragile, short-term material. Carmel, California, USA

The adobes used on the Carmel High School were waterproofed with asphalt emulsion, an experimental use of a waste petroleum product. There is evidence of only minor deterioration on the surface. Carmel, California, USA

Discovering the Carmel High School of adobe was a real surprise to me, when I learned of its existence in 1994 from one of my Elderhostel participants. He told me that as a young man he had helped build the school in 1938.

THE COMFORT FACTOR

Living in an adobe house generates a feeling that must have roots in some metaphysical connection with the earth. Recognized by all who have lived in an adobe home, it creates a sense of quiet, peace, and security. The softly flowing walls and rounded corners create a gentle, comforting, and secure feeling space. It is difficult to describe the feeling, other than to say it must be experienced to be recognized.

Another contributing comfort factor is the thermal "flywheel" effect. This is most noticeable in arid climates that have a wide daily temperature variation from day to night. The massive walls absorb and give off heat, which creates a stable indoor temperature with minor variations in any 24 hour period.

A debate has been raging for many years about the "insulation" value of adobe. On the one hand, some say that the insulation value is poor. On the other, the pro-adobe faction says this must be wrong because it is so comfortable, warm in the winter, and cool in the summer. Recent large scale tests have shown that both are right. If we have an outdoor temperature of 90 degrees f. in the daytime, and 60 degrees f. at night, the indoor temperatures will tend to average the extremes to approximately 75 degrees f. The variation inside during a 24 hour period will only be a few degrees. So: when we enter an adobe building in the daytime with a temperature of 90 degrees f. outside, it is only 75 degrees f. inside. Feels cool!. At night when we come in from outside at 60 degrees f., it still is 75 degrees f. Feels warm! The average is not quite that precise, and it represents the temperatures of several days ago. Extra thick walls may represent the average of two weeks ago!

The world faces a critical shortage of both housing *and* energy in the coming decades.

Solutions proposed by our current group of professional architects, engineers, and planners often fail to consider earthbuilding as a viable alternative.

The housing shortage and the energy shortage are more closely linked than we may realize. Most energy studies have concentrated on the economy and efficiency in the cost of heating and cooling buildings, but there is another dimension. What we're starting to look at, is the energy that is required to *manufacture* the everyday building materials we use. An extensive study done by an Architectural firm in New York, and at the University of Illinois Urbana-Champaign, determined the production and delivered energy costs of most common building materials. The energy costs were quoted in BTUs (British Thermal Units). As an example, for most of us non-scientists, 125,000 BTUs is a meaningless value. In practical terms, it represents the energy contained in one gallon of gasoline or diesel fuel. That is a quantity that we can visualize. It takes the energy contained in one gallon of gasoline to make eight common building bricks. It takes almost four gallons of gasoline for each bag of Portland cement. Lumber might be seen as energy free, because it grows using solar energy, but by the time usable boards reach the building site, the energy cost is more than six gallons for the lumber to build *just the frame* for a wall 10 ft. high x 10 ft. long. In addition to the energy expense for lumber used, ecological considerations discourage the cutting of trees for lumber around the world. One way the construction industry is meeting this challenge is by using lightweight

CONCLUSIONS

steel members for frame construction. Unfortunately, the study did not include the energy cost of sun dried adobe, but a comparison is made on the following page:

Based on this study, if we visualize a building wall ten feet high and ten feet long, (100 sq. ft.,) the following energy costs for the material to build only the framework are incurred:

❖ Built of wood 2"x 4"s = 785,000.0 BTUs = 6.28 gallons of gasoline

❖ Built of Steel Studs = 2,733,495.0 BTUs = 21.87 gallons of gasoline

❖ Built of adobe* = 2 man days = only perspiration

*Hand made, on site from site materials. This is a complete shelter wall, and needs no other covering or insulation to be complete.

Adobe and other types of earth buildings are seen in many parts of the world as a symbol of poverty, and used only in arid, desert climates. They further have the impression that the first heavy rain storm will destroy them. As we've seen in both instances, nothing could be further from the truth.

Many people have the impression that "if it's built of adobe, it has to look like the Santa Fe Plaza." Most people don't realize that adobe is a brick, and can be used for almost any architectural style. It has been proven time and again that earth buildings have been adapted to almost every climate, and that virtually no energy is required.

OF COURSE THERE ARE BETTER MATERIALS THAN ADOBE.

BUT AT WHAT COST?

In times of economic stress and hardship, people everywhere have turned to adobe to meet their needs. It's time to look back to our past for solutions! They are there!

chapter five
The Adobes of Latin America

Before the Spanish conquest of the Americas, many forms of earth construction had been in use for centuries. In areas where society had reached complex political levels, sophisticated architectural forms, features, and scientific principles were developed. Large irrigation projects and massive monuments were built by various religious and political organizations. In some instances, sun dried mud bricks may have been required as a form of tribute, enabling the rulers to construct huge monuments. In many cases, the bricks were not precisely sized, being shaped roughly by hand, without the use of molds. For the mud brick building technology of the time, the size and regularity of the product was not necessary.

PRE-COLOMBIAN TRADITIONS

The ruins of Chan Chan, a large prehistoric city, go as far as the eye can see. Only a small portion of the city has been excavated. Trujillo, Peru

Chan Chan was made up of a number of smaller communities or *barrios,* as they might be called today, and the city wall shown is only for this particular *barrio.* Trujillo, Peru

In the more remote areas, building technology was simple, like the pit house discussed earlier; while complicated architectural forms and a high degree of construction skills were developed in other parts of Latin America. Examples of these new skills often existed side by side with the older, simpler forms, displaying the wealth or class of the family. In spite of the lack of a written language, other than the pictorial glyphs, math and astronomy reached high levels.

Common features found in the Middle and Far East that never occurred in the Western Hemisphere were arches and vaults. There were big trees that would serve as structural members so it was not necessary to ponder the amazing concepts it took to conceive such elements as arches, domes, and vaults.

Chan Chan was a large city in the 12th century on the arid north coast where it seldom rained. Ample supplies of water were available for irrigation and family use from the substantial rivers that flowed from the nearby mountains to the Pacific Ocean. Trujillo, Peru

The *Hueca Dragón* (a small temple pyramid) is covered with designs carved in the adobe plaster. These wall carvings survived because of the very low rainfall. Sometimes it would not rain for thirty years. Trujillo, Peru

THE SPANISH INFLUENCE

When the Spanish conquistadors arrived, they brought many new ideas with them, and at the same time made use of local materials and skills. The vast distances from their customary supplies of building materials and skilled craftsmen made it necessary to make use of local custom, materials, and the craft skills of the people.

In some instances, the Spanish built their walls and buildings on top of the stone foundations that were still in place from of earlier civilizations.

The lower stone lower walls are from Inca buildings and their distinctive "crazy" coursing (see page 68) has survived for centuries. The Spanish made use of these as foundations by laying adobe walls above. Cuzco, Peru

chapter six

The Evolution of Adobe in New Mexico

The State of New Mexico is a living history book of the evolution of adobe from its most primitive beginnings to its adoption by modern society. In most parts of the world, people today tend to forsake known and familiar values of adobe in favor of new materials and technology. New Mexico is no exception, but tradition prevails. Santa Fe, one of the oldest cities in the United States, was originally an Native American community which the Conquistadors occupied and established as the first capital of New Spain in 1610. It was built entirely of adobe and native materials. With the acquisition by the United States and the arrival of the railroad in the 1880s, the then-popular Victorian and Greek revival influences were seen on the Santa Fe plaza.

A revolution to establish the unique sculptural qualities of adobe began shortly after World War I. The art-oriented communities of Santa Fe and Taos revere the adobe tradition and form. Today, the zeal for maintaining the "Santa Fe look" prevails in the form of building regulations. New construction must conform to the traditional patterns. A careful look behind the Pueblo style of the Santa Fe Plaza, however, reveals the Victorian form in disguise.

In spite of its detractors, New Mexico is the one place among industrial nations where adobe building is valued and honored as a premium building material. Most New Mexicans view adobe with a fond eye. However, there are strangers that not only view it with disdain, but with actual hostility.

NEW MEXICO IS THE LEADING USER OF ADOBE IN THE INDUSTRIAL WORLD

It is difficult for me to imagine why such unreasoned hostility occurs. Perhaps part of it is the imagined lower social strata in the mind of the hater. One time many years ago I submitted an application for a new adobe home to the architectural control committee of a self styled "upper scale" subdivision which was finally approved with some reluctance. It might also be related to the legendary failures of adobe buildings during earthquakes. In truth, every kind of un-reinforced masonry building tends to fail in earthquakes whether they are made of adobes or regular bricks. It is much more newsworthy to say that the "poor" adobes collapsed with many deaths. The term "adobe" adds some visual credence to the story. Additional research and technology has found that adobe is not the sole culprit in seismic failures.

When developing nations begin to address their housing needs, they look first at the most modern, efficient, and popular building materials available. Their professional architects, engineers, and building officials in most instances have been educated in Western institutions or at least by Western standards, so they have little knowledge of earth building technology. Unfortunately, the value, art, and charm of vernacular buildings are ignored or even despised as inferior, and little attention is paid to their time tested technology. The developing nations have come to the realization that they have no other choice than adobe. The world looks to the United States as the ideal standard, so it must look to New Mexico for information on adobe.

This simple, shabby appearing country house is where a family had been raised. The change in the masonry pattern indicates where a new portion of building was added sometime in the past for a larger family. It was bulldozed and replaced with a modern mobile home. What a waste! Los Chavez, New Mexico, USA

This spectacular historic Santa Fe home illustrates the extravagant side of the spectrum from the previous photo. Nearly all the wood items are hand carved in the traditional style. It is also fashionable to collect architectural element antiques to be built into new construction, giving an historical look. Santa Fe, New Mexico, USA

Curiously, adobe has a split image, particularly in New Mexico. One is poverty, where a poor person can build with the earth under their feet, buying nothing. The other is wealth, where opulence, sculpture, and art can prevail, but few can afford. Unfortunately, the most common world view of earth buildings, even among the householders, is poverty.

As little as thirty years ago, after World War II, adobe making in Albuquerque was a cottage industry. Arrangements had to be made in advance. When I started building with adobe, my most reliable source of adobes was an elderly man of more than 70 years, retired, who made adobes in his back yard. All I had to do was have several trucks of dirt delivered to his home and two months later he would have my thousands of adobes stacked neatly in his back yard. Now there are several highly mechanized adobe yards in New Mexico that can produce a large volume of adobes, and will deliver from stockpiles during the summer months of the year.

NEW MEXICO EARTH, an adobe yard, can make 6,000 bricks per day. It uses a soil mixing hopper with conveyor, a pug mill for faster mixing, and a soak pit used for temporary storage. The almost liquid mud is transported to the waiting forms with front end loaders. Albuquerque, New Mexico, USA

A study done by Edward Smith, a geologist, and Dr. George Austin of The New Mexico Bureau of Mines and Mineral Resources, found that in 1981, there were at least 54 adobe producers in New Mexico, who made more than eight million adobes. The majority of these were small and medium size producers, who often made adobes for their own use or for a particular project. Some of the bricks produced were for garden walls, some for repairs and additions.

There are many variable factors in estimating the quantity of adobes required for a particular plan, but an "average" adobe home of 2,000 square feet may require 5,000 adobe bricks. If all the eight million bricks were used for new homes, that would represent 1,600 homes. Samples were taken from most manufacturers and tested for strength. Although there was some variation in quality, nearly all samples were adequate for use.

The adobes of New Mexico represent a symbol and a way of life. It has been home to nearly all the simpler technological developments of adobe. The material and the simple styles persist. New developments in the mechanization of production and use of adobe in New Mexico are on the cutting edge of the technology. The world looks to New Mexico to find out how to do it best.

When the Spanish Conquistadors came to the new world, they found a number of sophisticated communities with well-established political patterns and forms of housing. Since the Conquistadors did not have the materials and tools that were common to them at home, they had to make use of native materials and skills. Adaptation was the rule, and they followed the lead of what the local people did. It was logical, the result of centuries of trial-and-error development, and it worked. Simple and logical were the governing factors, finely tuned to the environment. The technology made use of the materials most readily at hand, and utilized the labor and tools that were available. The style of simple battered walls (thicker at the bottom on the outside), protruding *vigas* (roof beams), and hand carved wood became the Pueblo style.

Some architectural historians have created sub-classifications such as "Pueblo revival," "Spanish colonial," and others, but essentially it is a simple style.

THE INDIAN HERITAGE

A typical street scene at Taos Pueblo. The mud plastered walls are repaired with mud by the women every few years as required. Notice the careful drainage pattern between the buildings. Taos Pueblo, New Mexico, USA

The Conquistadors brought with them the type of house plan where blank exterior walls were presented to the outside for privacy and security. The focus was directed inwards to patios and enclosed spaces. The Native American pueblos of the southwest were also built in a defensive pattern so that attacks could be repelled from an upper platform. The two patterns were very similar. Making use of the Indian skills in building was a logical consequence.

THE SPANISH INFLUENCE

The blank wall with the *zaguan* (gate) is typical. The gate is large enough for wagons and livestock, with an integral smaller gate for individuals. Martinez House, Taos, New Mexico, USA

The blank outer wall encloses one or more *plazuelas* (patios). Martinez House, Taos, New Mexico, USA

The *horno* fireplace built in a corner warms the heat storing adobe walls. Martinez House, Taos, New Mexico, USA

The territory of New Spain was a long way from the supplies and influence of Mexico City to the south, so the Spanish modes of building made use of the technology of the Native Americans. Servants and slaves were a common feature of wealthier households, so most articles were hand made, including building elements for homes. The technical process of building was simple and familiar to all because it was a family affair. Starting with a one room building, additional rooms could be added as needs increased with larger families or relatives. If the extra space was not needed, it was put to other uses or ignored, and it returned to the earth.

Adobe is the ultimate expression of ecology and conservation. The supplies of material are unlimited, automatically recycle themselves, and do not deplete our exhaustible resources.

**THE AMERICAN
INFLUENCE**

When the American influence began to be strongly felt after acquisition of the territory, the traditional plans of the Spanish gave way to less defensive needs. The family life-styles of the American settlers were also under transition from a dependence on servants and slaves to a more independent, self sufficient attitude. The Industrial Revolution in the east was becoming established, and certain architectural styles were popular at that time. Particularly admired was the Greek Revival style, and these influences were brought west by the settlers. The Greek Revival style was emulated in window and door frame decoration. Most of these had to be crafted by hand of wood.

The formally detailed entry door and triangular pediments of the American Territorial style over the windows are mixed with the Pueblo style projecting *vigas* and rounded parapet. A residence by John Gaw Meem, Albuquerque, New Mexico, USA

THE RAILROAD ERA

Another influence was the railroad era of the 1880s, which made possible the transportation of factory-made building materials from the east. Doors, windows, and millwork could be shipped by rail. The popularity of the Victorian style was a major influence also, with its ornate shapes and elements more readily available from the east. Even heavy, locally made articles like bricks needed a viable cheap transportation system which local railroads made possible. Railroad building was the business of the day and New Mexico had a large network of rail lines, most of which have disappeared.

The Americans developed a solution to one repetitive task caused by the vulnerable nature of adobe to rainfall. Vertical surfaces let the rainfall run off without much penetration, but the flat tops of the wall let rain soak in and were much more vulnerable. It was necessary to rebuild the top of the adobe walls each year because the parapets eroded at a very rapid rate. Their solution was to use fired bricks which would not erode. These were placed in the form of a decorative cap, the patterns of which became an art form of its own.

The Shed Restaurant is a good example of the use of the fired brick copings topping the walls. Other more elaborate patterns were common, and this feature became one of the trademarks of the territorial style. Santa Fe, New Mexico, USA

Local brick factories, while not common, produced a "sand" brick that was of poor quality, but somewhat more durable than adobe. A similar product called "burned adobe" is still available in many parts of Latin America, where they make many types of roofing and flooring tiles. "Burned" adobe (adobe that has been fired in a relatively low temperature kiln) is less subject to erosion, but it will readily absorb water, so its use in a climate where freeze and thaw cycles occur is not practical. The melting snow soaks into the bricks during warmer daytime temperatures and expands when it freezes at night so the bricks can be destroyed in a few winter seasons. In less severe climates in Latin America, it is still an important building material. The same simple process makes floor and roofing tiles.

The years before World War II were a period of consolidation of earlier expansions in New Mexico, and building was relatively dormant until World War II. During this period, with its economic ups

PRE-WORLD WAR II

and downs, adobe kept its place as a building material. Many buildings were made of wood, stone, and fired brick, but adobe was always there if budgets were not adequate for more modern materials.

It was a common practice in Albuquerque during the 1920's to hire a crew to dig your basement and make adobes from the excavated dirt. Two tasks for the price of one. What a logical use of resources!

We must accept the idea that there are better materials for building than adobe. Some are stronger, longer lasting, and usually cost more. Stone or concrete, for example, are the most lasting in any climate, wet or dry. Every reputable architect or builder tries to build with the finest materials we can afford, but sacrifices sometimes must be made to achieve a goal.

Most professional architects, engineers, and building officials at this time were at least aware of the possibility of using this material if circumstances made it necessary. Several examples are still in use. The New Mexico State Fair buildings in Albuquerque were built of adobe by the Works Progress Administration during the depression of the 1930s. Adobe was readily available at very low cost, and given its labor-intensive nature, it afforded employment to many during bad economic times. While many of the old adobe buildings of the New Mexico State Fair have been razed to make room for new buildings and changed needs, a few still stand today.

A track-side warehouse has withstood train vibrations and weather since the 1920s. Gallup, New Mexico, USA

New Mexico State Fair "Palomino" stables built of adobe by the WPA during the 1930s. Several State Fair buildings of adobe are still in use. Albuquerque, New Mexico, USA

Very few buildings at the University of New Mexico were initially built of adobe. The original building, Hodgin Hall, was built of brick and in a Victorian style. This was later modified to a Pueblo adobe style, and set the standard for the unique architectural style for the campus that prevails today.

The first building of the University of New Mexico, Hodgin Hall, was originally designed and built in a Victorian style. Albuquerque, New Mexico, USA. Historic Photo Courtesy of UNM Zimmerman Library Archives.

University of New Mexico's Hodgin Hall in 1995. The massing of its block elements evokes images of Taos Pueblo. Albuquerque, New Mexico, USA

Today this unique architectural style is one of the University of New Mexico's most outstanding features. A number of homes built by the faculty on the campus were adobe, and most in the Pueblo style. With the rapid expansion of UNM after WW II, they were purchased by UNM as they became available, and many are now serve as offices for various UNM Departments.

University of New Mexico visitor center, built of adobe, was originally one of the faculty homes. Albuquerque, New Mexico, USA

The "Kiva" style building, now called the "*Estufa*" (or stove), built by President William G. Tight and students around 1906, is a copy of the Kiva at Santa Domingo. A Kiva is a round religious meeting place, frequently underground and entered through the roof, and is common in our Native American pueblos. A local fraternal group of that time, The Yum Yum Society (a group that ate together, with aspirations of joining a national fraternity), in collaboration with President Tight, designed and built it and used it for meetings. Later the group became a chapter of Pi Kappa Alpha, a national fraternity, who still lease it from UNM.

The "Estufa" and the earlier central heating plant for UNM may have sparked the trend for the Pueblo Style architectural theme that the University of New Mexico campus is known for today. The "Estufa" is located on the East side of University Boulevard, one block North of Central Avenue.

Pi Kappa Alpha *Estufa*, a fraternity meeting place, built in 1906, still serves ceremonial purposes for the fraternity. UNM Albuquerque, New Mexico, USA

Another example of the logic of using adobe was demonstrated by a home building program by the WPA. This building program was established to assist and relocate farmers who had been devastated by the drought and depression of the 1930s. The WPA built small homes using adobe and local semi-skilled labor on irrigated tracts of land in the Rio Grande River valley at Bosque Farms, south of Albuquerque. More than forty homes were built in Bosque Farms, all but two of which are sound and still occupied. Rammed earth homes were built in other states where the climate was not suitable for making sun-dried adobe bricks.

It seems strange that in view of past successes with adobe, current government policies today are prone to limit its use as a home building material.

These farm homes were built by the WPA to serve farmers relocated by the massive drought of the 1930s. Nearly all are still in use. Bosque Farms, New Mexico, USA

These WPA homes were all built to a standard pattern and a number of owners have made additions to the original buildings. Bosque Farms, New Mexico, USA

The homes were rented to the tenants with an option to purchase. Most families purchased the property. Nearly all of these homes are in good condition and still occupied.

POST WORLD WAR II

When World War II ended, increasing populations created pressure for new housing. This was felt strongly in the Southwest, as many of the military personnel whom had been stationed here wanted to return. The home building industry, steady but not particularly robust before the war, came to life with a bang. New products like pumice concrete, aluminum, and plastics were favored, and project developments appeared everywhere. The demand was so strong that almost anything available sold immediately. Terrible dust storms from the disturbed soil sandblasted car windows and paint, leading to enactment of dust control ordinances. The undisturbed desert is relatively dust free except for the dirt roads, but when the land is graded and disturbed, the wind moves the top soil back and forth.

Striving to meet market demands, many of the builders made a great discovery. The Pueblo style with rounded wall tops and a minimum of decoration, emulated the popular Santa Fe style and could be built very economically. Pueblo style was easily copied, using frame wall construction. Four plain walls, flat roof, and minimum decorative elements echoed the traditional Pueblo style architecture, with a few projecting fake *vigas*. The *vigas* are round beams, (trees with the branches and bark removed) which support the roof in traditional Pueblo style. The spaces between the *vigas* are covered with boards or smaller peeled poles called *latillas*, and sometimes plastered. Most people accepted the traditional charm of the adobe look-alikes without really knowing the difference. One developer marketed a "super authentic" design, which had *vigas* protruding on all four sides!

The Pueblo style was eagerly used by mass housing developers because of its simple design details and low cost. The protruding *vigas* of traditional styles are used on all four sides here, illustrating a lack of understanding of this distinctive style. The angled walls at the corner represent battered sloping walls. Albuquerque, New Mexico, USA

The building industry underwent serious changes during the explosive expansion immediately following World War II. The pent-up demand for housing led to specialization of subcontractors. Speed of construction and low price were the main considerations. Most of these developers were not builders, but brokers, who assembled groups of subcontractor specialists producing a dwelling efficiently and rapidly.

New products, electric tools, and labor saving devices and materials prevailed, and most developers emphasized popular market gimmicks such as intercoms and central vacuum systems, rather than quality construction. A few of the traditional skilled builders continued to produce quality construction, but very few built with adobe. There were several good reasons for this. Adobe bricks were not readily available, and had to be ordered weeks or months in advance. The supply and price was uncertain. A great deal more hand work is necessary using adobe, taking longer to complete, so this conflicted with the market requirements for speed.

Most of the true adobe construction at this time was carried on by a few individuals in the market place, perhaps oriented more to art than speed, but they made up only a small percentage of the total. Traditional rural builders carried on as usual. Building methods for adobe do not work well with most conventional construction practices, where crews of specialists can be organized to work the job in an orderly sequence. Adobe building requires a lot of hand labor. A builder's crew may be masons in the morning, carpenters to set doors and windows in the afternoon, and then back to brick or concrete work. Most of the new builders wanting to build with adobe had to learn the craft either by trial and error, or from other adobe builders.

chapter seven
The Industry Today

The people of the world are rediscovering adobe, perhaps not so much because of their recognition of its aesthetic and practical worth, but because they have no other choice. New Mexico leads the world in the earthen building technology revival, because it is the only area in the industrialized world where adobe is regarded as a status symbol. A quick trip around the world shows the breadth of the industry and the parallels New Mexico has with the rest of the world. Similarities are obvious in brick making methods, techniques for building, and the appearance of the finished product. Buildings all begin to look alike.

A contemporary adobe home in the Manzano Mountains. P. G. McHenry, Architect. Tijeras, New Mexico, USA

A typical street scene that could be duplicated almost anywhere in Latin America. Most rural construction in Bolivia is done by the owner, using locally available materials that are free for the taking. The cash outlay for a building project is mostly limited to doors, windows, and hardware that the owner cannot make for himself. Punata, Bolivia

The *Souk,* or public market, in this town on the edge of the Sahara Desert, is typical of adobe construction common to North Africa. Mud plaster frequently is used to cover the sometimes roughly laid adobe bricks. Mud plaster can be easily renewed or refinished merely by dampening the surface and brushing it smooth with a sheepskin. Gabes, Tunisia

This Mediterranean town overlooking the old Roman ruins of Carthage has been restored, and is a popular tourist attraction. The project won the Aga Khan Award for restoration. Sidi Bou Said, Tunisia

A typical village scene in one of the older villages of Iran. Kerman, Iran

An old hacienda that has been modernized to meet today's standards. Puebla, Mexico

Today's economics dictate multiple uses for buildings wherever possible. In this active seismic area this small school was designed to be earthquake resistant, and also to serve as a public *Mercado* on weekends. Tlaxcala, Mexico

There are a number of adobe builders active today in New Mexico, many more than in the early years after World War II. Adobe has now become more fashionable which, unfortunately equates with more costly. Actually, it isn't the adobe part of the building that is so costly, but the accouterments that go with it. Larger foundations, special window and door treatments are needed to accommodate the thick walls. If we have adobe, then we probably must have plaster, which is more expensive than drywall made with gypsum. All of the hand-crafted finishing touches, like ceramic tile that one comes to expect in an adobe home, are time consuming, and add to the cost. To professional builders, any delay is costly, and in most cases, customer schedules must be met as promised. Building codes sometimes require treatments that are not necessary for good building. For example, adobe buildings of two or more stories are found throughout the world, but our Uniform Building Code prohibits any use more than one story tall. The State of New Mexico recognizes this lack of understanding and has a more liberal code for adobe.

Most of today's adobe builders are artists, and their clients are willing to wait the extra time required for them to complete the project. In some cases, the builders try to create an artistic piece of sculpture that can be lived in. Each room and vista offer new visual surprises and eye-pleasing forms. If the builder does not want the constraints, input, and limitations imposed by a client, the builder markets the home as art after it is finished. Depending on the reputation of the builder, both speculative and custom building seem to be successful.

A number of the merchant builders or brokers would like to enhance their product without the additional complications of an all adobe home, and so use "adobe accents." In some cases, the lengths that are required to make a "look alike" adobe may cost more than the real thing. Some clients scorn the adobe look, or idea, and want to follow a more currently popular trend. All things considered, whatever the preferences, the owner gets what he wants, the builder fills a need, and the artist creates art. If the economics work, all is well.

CONTEMPORARY USE

An outstanding current example of resources coupled with need was demonstrated recently with the completion of *La Capilla de Todos los Santos* in San Luis, Colorado. San Luis is located in south central Colorado, near the New Mexico border. San Luis, an economically depressed rural community, wanted to have a noteworthy church. The skills of Arnie Valdez, an intern architect, and the determination of the townspeople and the parish priest made their dream come true. Using traditional vaulting techniques, this shows what can be done with adobe.

Vaults (domes and arches) built of masonry, are becoming almost a lost art with many of the older construction skills in the United States. This skill is being revived here. *La Capilla de los Todos Santos*, San Luis, Colorado, USA

Located on a hill overlooking the valley below, *La Capilla* is a striking landmark. San Luis, Colorado, USA. (Photos Courtesy Arnie Valdez, San Luis, Colorado)

Adobe must have an important place in the future, for reasons of energy, if nothing else. It has been said that more than 50% of the world's population today live in houses built of earth. It would be difficult to corroborate that statement. We do know, however, that almost all housing on a worldwide basis had its roots in some type of earthen building. Ideas, patterns, and construction techniques were developed in response to needs. Modern materials and methods have become the standard, often ignoring traditional materials and techniques. Why should we not look to earthen buildings for the future?

Energy is the main reason adobe must be an important material of the future. Conventional building materials require a surprising amount of energy for their manufacture. For example, it requires the energy equivalent of one gallon of gasoline to manufacture eight common red bricks. One bag of cement represents more than four gallons of gasoline or diesel fuel.

FUTURE

This graphic illustration shows in vivid terms the energy required to make ordinary building bricks. One gallon of gasoline is required to make eight bricks. Albuquerque, New Mexico, USA

Imagine how many gallons of fuel are represented in the modern brick home. Adobe bricks, or rammed earth walls, on the other hand, require very little. Adobe bricks, made by hand, without special equipment, are virtually energy free, other than the perspiration of the brick maker. The sun provides the energy. If waterproof adobes are needed, and this is seldom necessary, they can be manufactured in a yard with labor saving machinery, adding asphalt emulsion, and our gallon of gasoline will still make fifty adobes.

Most energy today comes from fossil fuels which are limited in quantity. Our increased awareness of ecological problems and solutions require more stringent steps than have been necessary in the past. It is true that there are better, stronger or longer lasting materials with which to build than adobe, but can we afford them? Hard economic times of the past have demonstrated the viability of earthen building, and they will again one day.

WORLD UNDERSTANDING

People the world over have common bonds. The basic concerns are the same: love of family, adequate food, and shelter. While customs, traditions, and details vary from country to country, a common thread through time has been earthen housing. As we develop new materials and technology, some of the traditional values get lost or pushed aside, but the one that prevails is the urge to create shelter. The instinct to create shelter is one of the basics, ranking only after food. Children do this on a play basis, but as we become adults the dream gets lost in the complications of everyday life.

Dealing with the shortage of housing on a worldwide basis staggers the imagination. Why could this not be a common thread where needs, concerns, and activity enables strangers to communicate on common ground? The artisans that are skilled in earthen building could and should be encouraged. In Japan, skilled artists are honored as national treasures. Perhaps we should follow their lead. An exchange program between our people and those of other countries could create stronger bonds of understanding. The basic roots and demands are the same the world over. If the United States of America is regarded as the pinnacle of development by less fortunate countries of the world, we can share our modern science, tempered by the common traditions of the past centuries. We must make progress toward closer human understanding.

In our pursuit (perhaps worship might be a better choice of words) of modernity and current fashion, we have lost not only the skills and tradition but the initiative to do things for ourselves as well. Perhaps the traditional values of honesty, morality, and labor have been diminished at the same time as the technology. If we can become aware of, learn, and share even a few of these skills, perhaps it will start a reverse of the trend we are experiencing.

Columbia

Equador

Peru

Brazil

Chan-Chan
Trujillo

Andes Mountain Chain

Lima

Pacific
Ocean

Machu-
Picchu
Cuzco

Andes Mountain Chain

Bolivia

Andes Mountain Chain

Peru

chapter eight
Tour the Adobes of Peru

Great civilizations of Peru had come and gone long before the Spanish plundered the gold of the Incas. Ruins of these enormous monuments still give testimony to the building skills and the political organization that made it possible to organize the efforts of thousands of people to build such monuments.

Peru is a land of contrasts. The western coastal plains between the mountains and the shore of the Pacific Ocean are dry and desert-like, but with generous streams running from the mountains to the sea. This provided an ideal environment for building with earth: an adequate supply of water for living and irrigation, but with minimum rainfall to affect the adobe structures. Some areas of the coastal plain have had rain only every 30 years. The ruins with their carved mud decorations are breathtaking.

The town of Trujillo on the Pacific coast north of Lima is a prime example, with a number of major ruins nearby. The monumental ruins of Chan Chan are so large that only a small fraction of them have been investigated archaeologically, and an even smaller percentage have been restored.

TRUJILLO: CHAN CHAN

High massive walls separated
individual communities in
Chan Chan. Vast ceremonial
plazas with ramps are found
in many places. Chan Chan,
Trujillo, Peru

Carved decoration on the
mud plastered walls depicted
the sea and fish. Chan Chan,
Trujillo, Peru

Water from the mountain streams running to the sea was diverted into community ponds for domestic use and irrigation. Chan Chan, Trujillo, Peru

Carved decorations in the mud-plastered walls were caricatures of the common animals and fowl of the time. Chan Chan, Trujillo, Peru

LIMA   The city of Lima, on the coastal plain, is a modern city with modern architecture, interspersed with Spanish Colonial buildings, and one of the large pyramid sites, *Huaca* (holy place) Juliana. The relative size and scale of Huaca Juliania and other large community sites is emphasized by comparison with the modern city.

Huaca Juliana, is a large pyramid ruin almost surrounded by the modern city of Lima. The enormous size of the pyramid can be imagined from the relative scale of the city buildings. Lima, Peru

Adobe is in wide use today in many areas of Peru. In an area subject to severe seismic shock, it only follows that the Catholic University of Lima spends a large effort on seismic resistant building design. The adobe building art is more prevalent in rural areas, but is also popular in urban construction in smaller mountain cities

CUZCO   The city of Cuzco is one of the most outstanding examples of adobe use combined with the utilization of existing ruins. Cuzco is located in the heart of the Andes mountains at an elevation of 12,000 feet, and was the Inca capital for South America at the time of the Spanish conquest. Initially, it was built mostly with stone and had some remarkable features. It is difficult and expensive to transport materials such as cement and steel by road to Cuzco, so adobe is a primary material.

Anthony Crosby, a historical Architect with the USDI, National Park Service, inspects the Peruvian adobes. Adobes in Peru are much larger than the ones used in the United States. Cuzco, Peru

A new residence under construction using adobe and other traditional materials. Cuzco, Peru

Bamboo is relatively common in Peru, and is substituted for steel rebar (a rebar is a steel rod that is used to strengthen concrete and masonry). This strengthens the wall against earthquakes. Crushed, dried bamboo also replaces steel mesh used to reinforce plaster.

Street scenes of Cuzco, Mexico, and the southwestern United States are surprisingly similar. Granite, a very hard stone, was routinely used for walls and was shaped by hand using only stone tools. The stones were laid in what is termed "crazy coursing" with non linear horizontal joints. These could have offered a measure of protection from the earthquakes.

The Author, Paul McHenry, examines the pre-Colombian stonework. How the Peruvian people handled and shaped these stone blocks without metal tools is an unsolved mystery today. "Crazy coursing" may offer some seismic stability. Cuzco, Peru

The joints, so tight that a sheet of paper cannot be inserted between them, were all shaped with stone tools. This is the famous stone with eleven corners. Cuzco, Peru

The Spanish used the more easily worked (and more vulnerable) adobe bricks to build walls on top of Inca stone foundations. Instead of organic thatch for roofing, the Spanish introduced fired clay roof tile, still in wide use today. Most of the buildings in Cuzco follow the same pattern: Inca stone foundations, mud plastered adobe walls, and tile roof. Cuzco, Peru

Traditional roof construction includes wood rafters or beams covered with panels of *cana hueca*, a low strength bamboo, waterproofed with a layer of adobe soil and roof tile. Cuzco, Peru

Machu Picchu was built of stone rather than adobe, but it is such a monument to craftsmanship that it must be included in our tour.

The community went undiscovered until the early 20th century, and apparently was a ceremonial center rather than a living community. The almost vertical building site was implemented by the construction of stone terrace retaining walls, and provided vistas that are so breathtaking as to be almost beyond description.

MACHU PICCHU

The train track between Cuzco and Machu Picchu is at the bottom of the steep gorge of the Urubamba River. Cuzco, Peru

There is little arable land in the river valleys, so terraces were built on steep slopes to create narrow fields along the mountain sides. Machu Picchu, Peru

The multiple mountain-side terraces here can be seen on many of the mountain slopes. Machu Picchu, Peru

The pre-Colombian builders in Machu Picchu used stone, because it was readily available, and the mountains did not have the arid climate of the coastal cities. The size and quantity of buildings this high on the mountain is amazing. Machu Picchu, Peru

The stone terraces are an unusual feature by themselves. Peru is mountainous, with little arable land. To solve this, narrow terraces were built, using retaining walls on steep mountain-sides almost everywhere. The labor-intensive nature of such construction and farming is difficult to understand for farmers in more favorable conditions. The case for food production in Peru is the same as building: use whatever is at hand, and do whatever you have to do to make it work. The terraces can be seen rising to the top of very high mountains in many cases.

The painstaking original stone work can be seen in sharp comparison to the reconstruction work. Machu Picchu, Peru

The Experience of Machu Picchu is overwhelming. Machu Picchu, Peru

    While the Machu Picchu buildings are of stone rather than dirt,
the similarities in engineering and the awesome grandeur of the site
make it a significant stop on our tour.

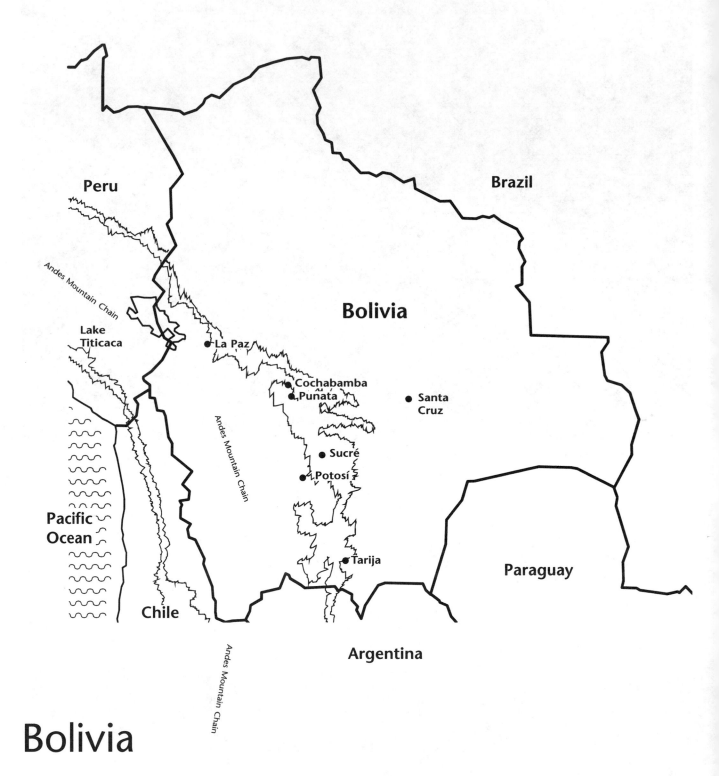

Bolivia

chapter nine
Tour the Adobes of Bolivia

The people of Bolivia have a somewhat different makeup and nature than Peru. Not as spectacular in terms of the Inca treasures, its mines nevertheless ultimately provided great wealth. The climate is varied from almost tropical on the eastern border with Brazil, to cold high mountain valleys in the central Andes. The largest city in South America during the mid 17th century was Potosi, a mining town with a reported population of more than 160,000.

This is a typical street scene in Cochabamba. Most of the buildings are two or three stories, and the older buildings are built of adobe in the traditional manner. Cochabamba, Bolivia

A typical modern office/residence that served as the *Programma de Control de Chagas* office. This modern building was not built with adobe and demonstrates the trend to more modern materials. Cochabamba, Bolivia

The architecture of Sucre, still the legal capital of Bolivia, is Greek Revival. Sucre is the seat of the courts and legal system. Sucre, Bolivia

URBAN SETTINGS

Most of the commercial buildings in the smaller cities of Bolivia in the past were constructed originally of adobe brick. Many have been refurbished with a facade of modern materials and design, but the adobe origins of most buildings can be seen from the alleys.

Cochabamba, a commercial city high in the Andes, had nearly all of its older commercial buildings built of adobe. Contemporary buildings are of more modern materials.

Sucre, has been a city where most of the judicial activities took place. It was built in a very formal, more grand style of Greek Revival, using stone.

Potosi, at an altitude of 14,000 feet, was once the major mining center of Bolivia. Potosi was the location of the National Mint, reputedly one of the largest adobe buildings in the world. The story is told that the wealthy families in Potosi sent their laundry to Paris via sailing ship, as adequate facilities were not available locally.

Most small communities are located along the trade routes, actually, more like trails, which were designed for pack animals rather than the modern auto. Most older roads are only passable using four wheel drive vehicles. One bridge over a river was a spectacular piece of stone work, but was not wide enough for modern vehicles. The new truck highway from Sucre to Potosi had to be located several miles to the west.

A typical old trail to Potosi from Sucre. It works fine for pack animals, but not for today's trucks. Sucre, Bolivia

A suspension bridge has Victorian style stone towers, but is only wide enough for pack animals. Sucre, Bolivia

RURAL SETTINGS: QUECHA FARM DWELLINGS

A large percentage of the rural population are Quechua Indians, a native race of the Andes from pre-Colombian times. Under numerous changes in the land reform laws, much of the farm land has been broken up from large holdings into very small family plots, and has been returned to the Quechuas.

Each of these small farmers build adobe homes, made from materials that they can obtain locally, and usually with very little cash outlay. The only items requiring cash are doors, windows, and hardware. With this system, houses can be built for very little cash.

The remains of a former large landholder's adobe hacienda still stand. Punata, Bolivia.

A serious health problem in Latin America is Chagas disease. It is a blood parasite infection transmitted by night feeding, blood sucking insects called *vinchugas*. At the onset of the disease, it can be controlled and eliminated by medication, but after a few years it becomes resistant to almost everything, and is usually fatal within ten years. The *vinchugas* will feed on any warm blooded animal, including livestock and fowl. By custom, all of the family farm dwellings, animal pens, etc. are usually in close physical proximity, so that this disease can be spread rapidly.

The insect's habitat is in cracks and crevices of any structure, where they live and breed. The United States Agency for International Development (USAID) is sponsoring many programs to reduce or help eradicate the incidence of this disease. This is done through medical programs using insecticide spray, health education, and home improvement implementations to reduce the insect's habitat.

USAID assigned me the task of finding a way to reduce the insect's habitat in typical dwellings by analyzing the vernacular building details, and suggesting changes.

Fortunately, it was possible to demonstrate a method for closing cracks and crevices on the adobe walls by rubbing a wet sponge or sheepskin in a smoothing process known as "floating" the mud plaster surface. The cane ceilings, with multitudes of cracks and crevices, had been coated with gypsum plaster, or a false ceiling made of sewn grain sacks that had been suspended. Both of these methods were expensive, involved cash outlay, and were not effective. It was surprising to me that the builders, skilled adobe craftsmen, were not aware of this simple repair of mud plaster. By using these methods, the cracks could be substantially reduced using commonly available materials. The construction rehabilitation budget for each dwelling was reduced by 40 to 50%.

Although most earth building techniques are common all over the globe, certain traditional techniques have been developed for special problem areas. These can be effectively shared for the benefit of all.

Unfortunately, many international relief agencies do not have the practical experience to be aware of some of the simpler traditional solutions to building problems. USAID is to be commended for such an effective response with an unconventional solution.

A simple farm dwellings with few amenities. Punata, Bolivia

Pens for fowl and small animals are also made of adobe, and are in close proximity to the homes. Tarija, Bolivia

Country lanes with garden walls of adobe offer privacy and security for each farm compound. Tarija, Bolivia

Gypsum plaster might be the first choice for sealing these cane ceilings, but it is too costly and is difficult to repair. Another solution is a cloth canopy of plasticized grain sacks stretched across the ceiling. This is fragile and expensive. Using simple adobe plaster reduces the habitat for the disease carrying insects, is cost free, and may be easily repaired with more mud. Tarija, Bolivia

These women are building a new kitchen in the traditional style. Ovens made of adobe are common worldwide. A fire is built in the oven, and once heated, the coals are removed and replaced with the food for baking. Tarija, Bolivia

Roof tiles are made with the same basic material as the adobe bricks, mortar, and plaster, with the possible difference of a slightly higher clay content. They are fired in simple kiln, using Eucalyptus leaves for fuel. Frequently, children are employed. Cochabamba, Bolivia

The building details are almost identical to those used in adobe building in the United States and Mexico. Wood timbers are used and roof beams, with ceiling/roofing panels woven of *Cana-Hueca* are laid across the beams. This is topped with a layer of thatch and covered with a thick layer of adobe mud to provide waterproofing. If and when the home-owner can afford it, the mud roof is further covered by fired roof tiles.

Placing a tile roof on the home represents a major effort for the farmer. The construction is performed by the whole family. Tarija, Bolivia

U.S. building codes call for a reinforced bond beam at the top of the adobe walls to support the roof structure and to provide a "collar" beam connecting all of the adobe walls. In Bolivia this is omitted, and a wooden brace steadies the two long walls of the building.

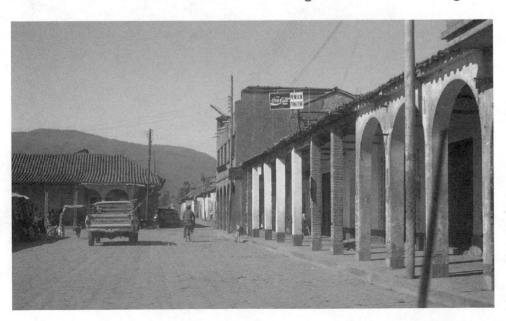

Small rural communities serve as trading centers and are similar in appearance. Punata, Bolivia

In the mountains between Sucre and Potosi, several remote villages with only primitive roads are beneficiaries of aid programs to help with health and home improvement projects. In some instances, the materials chosen for building were not suitable, not because of their quality, but because of secondary factors. An example was the use of corrugated iron roofing to replace adobe and tile. Successful use of corrugated iron depends on a satisfactory fastening system. The irregular sizes and shapes of the supporting beams made this impossible. In addition, the tin roof provided no insulation value, and when re-used, had holes from earlier uses that leaked when it rained. The choice of materials and details can often be better served by evaluating and modifying local traditions.

The village church is frequently the center of village activities. Punata, Bolivia

Home-owners everywhere work continually to improve their homes. The Bolivian farmers are no exception, but most of their improvements are limited to what they can produce themselves without cash outlay. Tarija, Bolivia

This mountain community is served by both the original trails, and by the new truck highway. Firewood is collected as a cash crop for export to the large cities. Laja, Bolivia

The village of Villa Carmel, near Cochabamba, has a unique form of mud brick domes, reportedly the only ones in the Western Hemisphere. The only comparable building forms are cone shaped structures built near Lake Titicaca on the northern border.

The rectangular building forms are common, but the round dome form is unique. Villa Carmel, Bolivia

Although a detailed examination of this building was not possible, it appears that it might be a "corbelled" dome as opposed to the "vaulted" form found in the Middle East. Villa Carmel, Bolivia

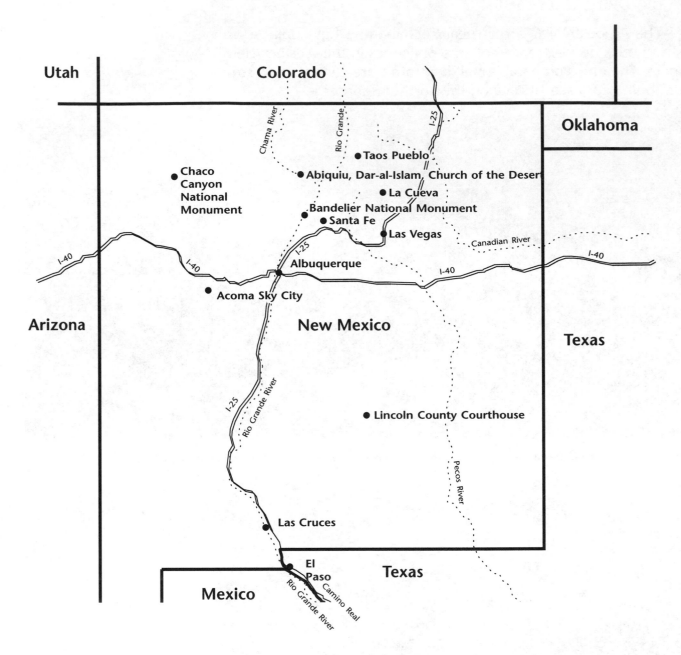

New Mexico

Tour the Adobes of New Mexico

History is alive in New Mexico. It is possible, in one day, to time travel from prehistoric scenes to the latest in modern science. We will take a pictorial tour of New Mexico, and then see how it compares with other parts of the world.

Chaco Canyon is one of the most outstanding archaeological sites in North America. It is in a remote location, more than 100 miles from the nearest major city (Albuquerque), and is frequently bypassed by the casual tourist. The valley has been occupied since earliest times, but the monumental ruins were built and occupied by the Anasazi as a major trading center dating from the 10th century AD. A number of other complexes were built in close proximity, and the area was subsequently abandoned in the 12th century. The causes for its demise are not known, but may have been the result of overpopulation and climatic change. While it is built primarily of stone in its later stages, it seems to have begun with adobe and masonry technology.

The word *Anasazi* means the Old Ones, and the origins of those early residents are not clear. Some indications are that they were migrants from the northwest over the land bridge from Asia, or they may have come from Meso-America to the south. I think the latter is the more likely.

CHACO CANYON

There are indications of two cultural levels that were living side by side at the height of Chaco Canyon's development. One is the pit house, a simple early phase, while other major ruins nearby reflect a great sophistication in design and construction technology. Some features indicate an extensive knowledge of astronomy.

Within Chaco Canyon, there are fifteen major ruins, demonstrating several distinct building skills. One is the use of dry stone masonry, relatively uncut and natural (Pueblo Bonito); and another of stones cut and shaped to resemble to resemble bricks (Pueblo del Arroyo). There is also an evolution of the masonry style, which is used by archaeologists to date the structures.

The evolution of masonry styles in Chaco Canyon is shown by the four distinct methods used in this museum exhibit. The bottom layer just uses large rocks and mud, and is the earliest. The next layer uses large rocks with tiny stones in between. The third layer uses small stones with wide band larger stones, and the top layer uses only larger stones. This beautiful masonry work was covered with mud plaster. Chaco Canyon, New Mexico, USA

This wall, made of stones shaped like adobes, differs from other methods that use broken stone pieces. Pueblo del Arroyo, Chaco Canyon, New Mexico, USA

The standing structures are very large, carefully planned, and built with skilled finishing techniques using stone and wood, far more complex than what might be needed for simple shelter. Wood for structural timbers came from nearby forests, or the valley may have been forested at that time, and lost later to over-cutting and drought.

There are other monumental centers that were contemporary with Chaco Canyon. One is Casa Grande in Arizona, and another is Casas Grandes in Chihuahua, Mexico. Both of those examples are primarily of earth, with minimal use of stone, but they all show similarities. My personal conclusion is that these builders came from Meso-America as traders, although what they were seeking is uncertain.

This wall originally had stone columns. The openings were later filled in. Similar forms are found at Casas Grandes, Chihuahua, Mexico, but were built with mud rather than stone. Chaco Canyon, New Mexico, USA

The resources of the area were minimal, some copper and turquoise, but the prosperity and size of Chaco Canyon seems much larger than would have been necessary to sustain such trade.

One other commodity that might be considered would be slaves, which could be transported and sold in Meso-America, in the manner of slave traders who went to Africa. During the collection and waiting time for a caravan, it could have been possible and desirable to train the slaves in building skills. A skilled slave would have more value, and perhaps the unskilled ones would have value as sacrificial victims, an additional food source. Bernal Diaz, Cortez' chronicler, stated that the defenders of Mexico City shouted that they would kill them and eat their flesh.

Original ceilings of peeled poles are done with great care, indicating an insistence on great skill or a lot of time available to achieve such careful detailing. Chaco Canyon, New Mexico, USA

BANDELIER NATIONAL MONUMENT

Bandelier National Monument is a large group of archaeological ruins near Santa Fe, on the eastern side of the Jemez Mountains. The Jemez Mountains were formed as a strato-volcano, which deposited large quantities of volcanic ash in the vicinity. The resultant erosion of these ash deposits created canyons in the solidified ash, a soft stone called *Tufa*. Pockets in the steep canyon walls have been naturally eroded by wind and weather . *Tufa* is soft and easily shaped with a tool as simple as a stick, so existing caves and pockets can be easily enlarged to make larger rooms. Natural openings were supplemented by additional masonry structures built onto the cliffs. The living sites chosen were usually on south-facing cliffs, with good exposure to the winter sun. The Rio Grande River circles the eastern edge of the Jemez Mountains, and some sites have perennial streams flowing from the mountains to the Rio Grande River, supplying water year round.

There are thousands of archaeological sites in the Bandelier National Monument, most of which have never been thoroughly investigated. Frijoles Canyon and Puyé Cliffs are the among the larger and more accessible sites. The origins of the people who fashioned homes from the soft *tufa* cliffs are not precisely known, but they may be descendants of the people who abandoned the Chaco Canyon area. Another feature of Frijoles Canyon, separate from the cliff structures, is *Tyuonyi*, (pronounced TWON-YEE), which was built in a circular pattern on the valley floor. It is interesting to note that the *Tyuonyi* structure, at the bottom of a steep walled canyon that one might expect to be shady in the winter, is exposed to full sunlight even when the sun is at its lowest point on December 21.

FRIJOLES CANYON AND PUYÉ CLIFFS

Tyuonyi ruins on the bottom of Frijoles Canyon is a part of Bandelier National Monument. The circular shape encloses a central plaza and indicates a need for defense. This is a change of pattern from the cave dwellings. Frijoles Canyon, New Mexico, USA

Pockets were carved in the soft *tufa* stone cliffs to support roof beams for houses that enlarged the natural caves. Puyé Cliffs, New Mexico, USA

ACOMA

The name Acoma (now more commonly known as Acoma Sky City) appears on the earliest maps ever made of the southwest and has been a place where people have lived for more than 1,000 years. It is 50 miles west of Albuquerque on a sandstone *mesa* (table) rising more than 300 feet from a valley floor, and was oriented for defense. The houses are arranged in three rows of apartment style house blocks, some as high as three stories. The rows are oriented on a northeast-southwest axis to make use of morning sun and afternoon shade. The highest levels are located on the north side, providing terraces and outdoor living spaces on the south side. Solar oriented overhangs provide shade from the summer sun, and wind-walls provide privacy and shelter from the storms and wind. It is obvious that their living patterns were finely tuned to the climate. The Acoma people, like most other Indian Pueblos, are nominally Christian, but follow their own religious beliefs and practices as well. Sky City has no water or electricity, and relatively few full time residents, except during ceremonial celebrations. Most families live on the valley floor where regular utilities are available. The Acoma's want to keep Sky City free of modern amenities, so it can provide a tie to their old customs and traditions.

Each dwelling in Sky City is owned by the female descendants of each family and passes to the female descendants. An unusual feature discovered during some reconstruction was that there seldom are common walls between family units. In spite of the advantages of using one wall to be shared between dwellings, the Acoma's insist on their own wall. The wisdom of this becomes apparent in examining historical photos over the past 100 or more years. Individual houses show consistent patterns of neglect and decay, and then repair and renovation. If the family next door lets their home decay and the wall collapses, the neighbor has only to worry about his own wall. The collapse of a neighboring wall will not affect his family. Robert Frost also said "good fences make good neighbors."

The old sand dune trail was once the major access for traffic to Sky City. Visitors had to walk up the dune trail and supplies were taken up by horse drawn sledges. It has since been paved, but visitor vehicles are prohibited. There is a visitor's shuttle bus for tours. Acoma Sky City, New Mexico, USA, 1946

A typical street scene, with house blocks lined up to take best advantage of the south side sun exposure. Acoma Sky City, New Mexico, USA

TAOS PUEBLO   Taos Pueblo is perhaps the best known of the New Mexico pueblos because of its proximity to the major tourist centers. The pueblo is only a few miles northeast of Taos, and is well maintained by responsible leadership and skilled crews. In their community, the men do the construction and the women do the mud plastering, which has been developed into a fine skill. The pueblo welcomes tourists, an important source of revenue from visitor and photo fees and the purchase of arts and crafts made by the people of the pueblo.

The new church has been freshly painted and stuccoed, in sharp contrast to the pueblo. Taos Pueblo, New Mexico, USA

A traditional home may have a ladder for rooftop or terrace access and many also have internal stairways. Taos Pueblo, New Mexico, USA

RIO GRANDE RIVER PUEBLO

The Rio Grande Pueblos were settled from diverse origins, and have several language groups that are not related, but of distinctly different roots. At the time of the Spanish conquest, the people living in the pueblos had well-developed community, cultural, and political patterns, and used earth and local materials for their buildings. When the Spanish came, they made use of the local building methods and skills. Today, many of the people of the Rio Grande Pueblos are employed in local industry or traditional pueblo activities. A curious note is that when a building project is planned, the pueblo people do not always make their own adobe bricks but buy them from local large scale adobe producers. The production of adobe bricks takes hard physical labor, a large space, is time consuming, and is subject to loss from rainfall until the bricks are dry. At the San Juan Pueblo, north of Santa Fe, a mechanized adobe production yard was set up with the aid of government grants. After several years of operation the adobe making equipment was sold so a government financed industry would not be competing with the private sector. During this period, contract bricks were made for the Dar Al Islam group, who were building an Islamic community near Abiquiu. The new owner of the adobe making operation is now the largest producer of adobe bricks in the United States, making more than one million bricks per year to supply the Santa Fe area market.

RURAL SCENES   The major communities of Santa Fe and Taos were linked by the "high road to Taos" which gave life to the villages of Chimayo, Truchas, Peñasco, Las Trampas, and Ranchos de Taos, and was the principal route between Santa Fe and Taos. A more direct route would have been to follow the Rio Grande River, but the steep walls of the canyons and difficulty for wagons made necessary an easier, if longer route. Most of these village scenes have changed little from their earliest beginnings. Reliable water supplies were the most important considerations and irrigation patterns were established in the 18th century that are still in use today.

This country road was probably a portion of the old *Camino Real*, the road from Mexico City to Santa Fe. La Cieniga, New Mexico, USA

The La Cueva mill is a part of a small community on the Mora River, between Las Vegas and Ranchos de Taos. La Cueva, New Mexico, USA

The Monastery of Christ in the Desert stands against a backdrop of multi-colored sandstone cliffs. The stucco and stone echo the natural colors and textures. Abiquiu, New Mexico, USA

The mountain men trapping fur were the first European-Americans that visited Taos and Santa Fe, and then came cattle barons and mining camps. Traditional trade routes provided an opportunity for developing settlements in sparsely populated areas of New Mexico. During the 1880s when the railroads reached the area, many earlier trade centers along the old wagon roads were abandoned as new trade centers were established near the railroad. The town of Lincoln was the county seat until bypassed by the railroad. The town of Lincoln is a popular tourist attraction because of Billy The Kid and the Lincoln County cattle wars. Violence was common in Lincoln. The Lincoln County Courthouse, the Tunstall store, and many other buildings are intact and well preserved. The town has been kept in a remarkable state of preservation, and is a sort of time capsule, frozen in the 1880s. A large portion of the town buildings are owned by the New Mexico State Monuments Division of the Museum of New Mexico. The owners of the other buildings also help maintain the historic flavor of Lincoln.

The Lincoln County Courthouse was the center of several gunfights involving Billy The Kid and rival ranch factions. During one gunfight, the bodies lay in the street until some pigs escaped from their pen and started eating the corpses. Lincoln, New Mexico, USA. 1925 Photo courtesy of University of Arizona Library, Special Collections.

The Tunstall store was owned by one of the rival factions, and had wood window shutters reinforced with 1/4 inch steel plate so they were bulletproof. Lincoln, New Mexico, USA

EL CAMINO REAL

El Camino Real, or "The Royal Road," was the major route between Santa Fe and Mexico City. Most settlements were located in places with a perennial water supply which could be adapted for irrigation. The main route of the *Camino Real* in New Mexico followed the Rio Grande River, with the exception of a stretch of very rough terrain between present day Las Cruces and Socorro which was difficult for the primitive *carretas*. A *carreta* is a two wheeled cart with wood wheels, drawn by oxen. The wood wheels rubbing against the wooden axles made a terrible screech that was often described by earlier travelers. An alternate route east of the central mountain chain was established and called the *Jornada del Muerto* (Journey of Death). It had only one watering place in the 90 mile route, but was much smoother. All supplies for the settlements had to come from Mexico City and only a few trips were scheduled each year.

Under these conditions, most building supplies had to be made locally. The resulting hand crafted items such as doors, windows, and tools are highly prized today, and incorporated in restoration projects. When the southwest was under Spain's control, any traffic or trading with the United States was forbidden by the authorities. After the Mexican Independence in 1821, the same attitude persisted but traders on the Santa Fe Trail finally were allowed. Local authorities charged high tariffs on the goods imported, but in spite of this, trade was profitable for all concerned. It increased until the acquisition of the territory by the United States after the Mexican War (1846-1848). The Gadsden Purchase, a strip of land in southern New Mexico and Arizona finalized the present border between Mexico and the United States in 1853.

ABIQUIU

The town of Abiquiu, on the Chama River northwest of Espanola, was initially a *Genizaro* community. It was made up of the offspring of non-European parents of mixed blood and former prisoners of the Indians who had been recaptured or ransomed. These people were uncomfortable in other communities and formed their own. The Chama River provides good pasture and some irrigation.

DAR AL ISLAM MOSQUE

Dar Al Islam is an Islamic community originally established near Abiquiu to provide a living example of Islam in America. Supported by International Muslim groups, Dar Al Islam purchased property from a local rancher, Alva Simpson, who had holdings along the Chama river and extensive grazing lands. Hassan Fathy, a famous Egyptian architect, known internationally for his efforts to provide low cost adobe homes for the poor, designed the community which contains a mosque, *madressa* (religious school), and living quarters. Adobe, common in both New Mexico and the Middle East, was used in the construction, but in a Middle Eastern architectural style with domes and vaults. Technical complications arising from climatic differences between Egypt and New Mexico created some problems. The snow and cooler winters of New Mexico caused heating and moisture problems not found in the Egyptian climate. The design details have been modified to make it work.

The mosque at Dar Al Islam is designed in the traditional pattern of an Islamic community. The building elements are arches, domes, and vaults, principally those found in the Middle East. The *"claustra"* (triangular shaped openings in the wall) are for light and ventilation, but provide privacy. Abiquiu, New Mexico, USA

The interior of the mosque is divided into separate areas for men and women. The women's prayer area is located behind the wood screen. Abiquiu, New Mexico, USA

THE MONASTERY OF CHRIST IN THE DESERT

This monastery was founded by the Benedictine Order in 1964 at a remote location on the Chama River, northwest of Abiquiu. It can only be reached by fourteen miles of unpaved dirt road from U.S. Highway 84. The monastic church was designed by the Japanese architect George Nakashima. The church, in an unusual round plan, with four alcoves and a central altar, is covered by a high tower with large windows, through which can be seen the spectacular colored cliffs of the Chama River Valley. The adaptation of the adobe building to its site is breathtaking. Visitors are welcome and guest facilities for retreats are available.

The large, carved entrance doors welcome visitors into the quiet chapel. Abiquiu, New Mexico, USA

The large windows of the chapel display the colored cliffs and elegant setting. Abiquiu, New Mexico, USA

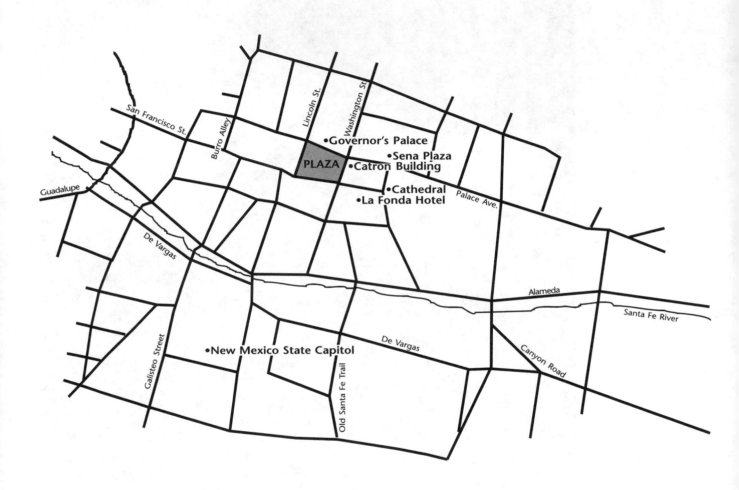

San Francisco St.

Burro Alley

Lincoln St.

Washington St

•Governor's Palace

•Sena Plaza

PLAZA •Catron Building

•Cathedral

•La Fonda Hotel

Palace Ave.

Guadalupe

De Vargas

Alameda

Santa Fe River

Galisteo Street

•New Mexico State Capitol

De Vargas

Canyon Road

Old Santa Fe Trail

Santa Fe

The Palace of the Governors in Santa Fe is reportedly the oldest government capital building or seat of government in the United States. It was founded (in its present location) in 1610 and served as the primary government building and residence of the governor, from the Spanish administration into the late 19th century. A well-known novel, <u>Ben Hur</u>, was written by New Mexico Governor Lew Wallace during the time he was governor, living in the Palace. In its early years, it functioned well as a fort, the three foot thick adobe walls being able to withstand most of the weapons of the time. During the Pueblo Rebellion of 1680, most of the Spanish settlers, and some of the Indians who had sided with the Spaniards were driven to Ysleta, south of El Paso. The rebelling Pueblos finally overcame the Palace fortress by diverting the stream which supplied the Palace with water.

An earlier capital had been founded near Alcalde, New Mexico, near the junction of the Rio Grande and Chama Rivers, about 35 miles to the north, near present day San Juan Pueblo. The roads of that time, or more accurately "trails," followed earlier trade routes established by prehistoric peoples, and streams with a dependable water supply. Santa Fe was built on the site of an earlier Indian pueblo.

> *The city street plan is laughably described as having been laid out by a boracho (drunkard) on a blind burro during a sand storm. Like most early communities, buildings were constructed along the paths that were used at the time. The street names, formalized at a much later date, still reflect this as "Old Santa Fe Trail," "Old Pecos Trail," etc.*

During the Victorian Period, architectural styles reflected the Greek Revival influence very popular about the time of the Civil War. Commercial buildings on the Santa Fe Plaza were done in this style.

In 1926, the Old Santa Fe Association vowed they would: "...preserve and maintain the ancient landmarks, historical structures, and traditions of Old Santa Fe, to guide its growth and development in such a way as to sacrifice as little as possible of that unique charm, born of age, tradition and environment which are the priceless assets and heritage of Old Santa Fe..."

Old photographs show a wood railing on top of the portal of the Governor's Palace. Ultimately, an ordinance was passed requiring that all new buildings in Santa Fe had to be in the Pueblo style and have the design reviewed by a special architectural committee. This requirement is still in place today. Subsequent remodeling of the commercial buildings on the Plaza covered up or disguised most of the Victorian influences of the past, but they can still be seen if one looks

SANTA FE: THE REVIVAL OF ADOBE

carefully. The Catron Building on the east side of the Plaza, on the corner of Palace Avenue, displays the Victorian brick on its upper stories, with the lower levels conforming to the Santa Fe style.

The Catron Building from the Victorian era has a portal done in the Santa Fe style. The arched window openings and dark brick of that period have been painted white to minimize the contrast between that and the Pueblo style buildings adjacent. Santa Fe, New Mexico, USA

The Governors Palace was the Capital for the province of New Spain, and all its subsequent inheritors until after the turn of the 20th century, when it was converted into a museum. Santa Fe, New Mexico, USA

Canyon Road, once a trail into the mountains to the east, is now a favorite tourist area with galleries and fine restaurants. Santa Fe, New Mexico, USA

Santa Fe today has become one of the most popular tourist destinations in the world. A boon to the local business people, it has been a double edged sword for some. The construction of large luxury homes, condominiums, and apartments have caused rapidly rising property values which, in turn, have increased property taxes to the point that the native Santa Feans cannot afford to live there.

Santa Fe streets are known for their unique character and charm. Most followed the water courses and irrigation ditches, and houses were built along these. The one shown here is named Acequia Madre (mother irrigation ditch). Santa Fe, New Mexico, USA

Santa Fe adobe home before re-stuccoing. Santa Fe, New Mexico, USA

Santa Fe home after re-stuccoing. Santa Fe, New Mexico, USA

This adobe home is given a new life and appearance with only a coat of stucco.

afterword

The American Association for International Aging and its Development Education for Retired Americans Project has been pleased to provide this exploration of adobe, one of our world's architectural and cultural treasures.

The United States has an important role to play on the world stage, and the players include our human, physical, and financial resources. *The Adobe Story: A Global Treasure* represents a positive approach to world relationships, and to our national goal of learning from as well as sharing with our global neighbors. It also provides an excellent model for combining world awareness with action.

The book provides countless illustrations of adobe as a global phenomenon, as practical in Europe, Asia, Africa and Latin America as it is in our own back yard. Americans have learned many adobe building techniques from other countries. Indeed, the very name adobe is traced to its Middle Eastern origins. As we have established our own traditions, we have contributed to the knowledge base about its use in architectural design, stabilization, and construction. Now, when we share this know-how with the world community, it carries the added value of our own myriad cultures and experiences.

The Adobe Mission Project discussed in the preface exemplifies our efforts to illustrate the relationship between domestic and international concerns. It represents an "acting locally thinking globally" program in which practical experience at home conveys a global reality. The origination of the model of combining intellectually stimulating education and practical community service came from the first adobe mission project.

The travelogue continues the theme of domestic and international experiences and relationships. The book itself is an international tour to some of the world's showcase examples of adobe building. In New Mexico the Church of the Desert and the Islamic mosque present contemporary images of what can be done when we add American technology to traditional art. Yet, the church was designed by an architect from Japan and the mosque by an architect from Egypt. The visits to the author's home state and to Peru and Bolivia provide evidence that no matter where we live or travel, in any state or nation - we can create our own adobe tour.

It is exciting to recognize things that we have in common with other lands, including the beauty, serenity, stability, and environmental advantages of adobe. As Americans, we continuously strive for new and innovative ways to meet the challenges of world citizenship. However, seldom do we think the challenge can be met with a story as old as *"The Adobe Story: A Global Treasure."*

Helen K. Kerschner, Ph.D.

list of illustrations

ADOBE BUILD-IT-YOURSELF, McHenry, P.G. Jr.
The University of Arizona Press, Tucson, AZ USA (Rev. Ed. 1985)
1973
9 X 12, 157 pp. ISBN 0-8165-0370-2
A comprehensive study on the technology of construction with
adobe for owner builders.

**ADOBE AND RAMMED EARTH BUILDINGS: Design and
Construction**,McHenry, Paul G. Jr.
University of Arizona Press, Tucson, AZ 1989 (Originally published
by John Wiley & Sons, New York 1984)
8.5 x 11, paper, 217 pp. ISBN 0-8165-1124-1
A definitive work on international earthen construction technology,
with data, properties, engineering, applications and alternative
construction details.

ARCHITECTURE WITHOUT ARCHITECTS: A Short Introduction to
Non-Pedigreed Architecture, Rudofsky, Bernard,
University of New Mexico Press, Albuquerque, NM USA 1987
(Originally published by the Museum of Modem Art, New York,
1965; also Doubleday & Co., New York, 1969)
8.5 x 9.5, 157 pp. ISBN 0-8263-1004-4 UNM Fine Arts
A worldwide trip to visit "home made" buildings.

ARIZONA RANCH HOUSES, Stewart, Janet Ann
The Arizona Historical Society, Tucson, AZ 1974
8 x 9, 121 pp.
Typical Arizona Ranch house designs

LA CASA ADOBE, Lumpkins, William T.
Ancient City Press, SANTA FE, NM 1961
10 X 14, 50 pp.
A collection of pencil drawings of beautiful adobe home plans, elevations and details.

OF EARTH AND TIMBERS MADE, Bunting, Bainbridge, and Lazar, Arthur
University of New Mexico Press, Albuquerque, NM 1974
8.5 X 11, 96 pp. ISBN 0-8263-0318-8
A collection of sensitive photos showing the art and culture of New Mexico homes, many from the 19th Century.

OLD SANTA FE TODAY, The Historic Santa Fe Foundation
The University of New Mexico Press, Fourth Ed. 1991
8.5 x 11, 79 pp. ISBN 0-8263-1305-5
A pictorial visit to many charming places in Santa Fe.

TAOS ADOBES: Spanish colonial and territorial architecture of the Taos valley.Bunting, Bainbridge; Booth; Jean; Sims; William R.
Museum of New Mexico Press, Santa Fe, NM 1992
(Originally published by the Ft. Burgwin Research Center, and the UNM Press 1964)
8.5. x 11 , Paper, 80 pp.
An in depth look at several historic adobe homes in the Taos area, with measured drawings and historic photos.

DOWN TO EARTH, Dethier, Jean
Thames & Hudson Ltd, London, UK 1965
8 x 9.5, 192 pp. paper ISBN 0-87196-800-2
Translated from the French by Ruth Eaten. Pictorials based on the Exhibion Des Architectures de Terre, initiated and directed by Jean Dethier and produced by the Centre Georges Pompidou, Paris, in collaboration with the Deutsches Architektur Museum, Frankfurt.